A License to Live

One man's journey to self-realization.

By Guy R. Ramsdell

ISBN 0-7414-3175-0

TXu1-261-720

Published by:

INFI∞ITY
PUBLISHING.COM

1094 New DeHaven Street, Suite 100
West Conshohocken, PA 19428-2713
Info@buybooksontheweb.com
www.buybooksontheweb.com
Toll-free (877) BUY BOOK
Local Phone (610) 941-9999
Fax (610) 941-9959

Printed in the United States of America

Printed on Recycled Paper

Published May 2006

Table of Contents

Chapter One

I'm standing in front of my father's old house; the new owners have picked up the keys. I am now homeless. How I got into this situation, well that's a story in itself. To make a long story short, bad things happened when I tried to work. They didn't involve the work itself, but the people with which I worked. I always showed up on time, and had no trouble doing what I was told, but the jobs never worked out for long. I didn't know then that the problem was me.

What this book is about is how I learned the truth about myself, served the Lord Jesus Christ, and coped. The time was July 1, 1990 to August 25, 1996. I was forty-seven years old at the beginning of this period.

I had this 73 Pinto runabout, (Hatchback) which I had taken the passenger seat out of in a previous adventure, and put in a board and pad. This was my bed, with my head resting on the dashboard.

My possessions are in the car, or in a friend of mines' attic. I have a PLAN. I will go to the Metolious River area of eastern Oregon, and get in shape to do a lot of walking. I drove to a campground called Monty, on the lower Metolious River. You could stay free for two weeks, then you had to leave for two weeks, and then you could come back. (It wasn't free when I was there last, in 1998.)

I did most of my hiking in the morning, and rested, read, or watched the chipmunks fuss with each other in the afternoon. Other diversions were the rafters, and kayakers that came down the river.

I haven't told you that I find things. The most notable item from this period was a Swiss Army knife. It had been run over several times, the corkscrew was gone, (I don't drink anyway!) and so were the plastic sides, but otherwise it was a useful tool. It is in my pocket as I write this. I had a pocket knife, and when I later lost it, the Swiss Army knife became it's replacement. PTL! I'm sorry for the person that lost it, but I had no way of returning it.

I had situations to keep an eye on, and so had to go and check the mail periodically. It was forty or more miles to the closest Post Office. I got groceries and water there as well. There was no drinking water at the campground.

After my first stay there I went to a sort of re-treat/reunion combination in Newberry Crater, near Paulina Oregon. This was under the auspices of Ecola Hall Short Term Bible Studies, or Ecola Hall. They use the facilities of Cannon Beach Conference Center, in Cannon Beach, Oregon. I had a nice time, made some new friends, and came back with some unexpected passengers. Mice! They apparently expected to spend the winter and eat my food too! I got rid of one of them in Bend Oregon, when one of them ran out, when I stopped for gas. The attendants and I chased it, and I was about to stomp it, when one of the attendants, (Girl) said, "Don't crush it, it's cute." The other attendant caught it and put it in a jar. I finally caught the other one with a mousetrap, but not before it had destroyed some of my granola cereal. I had to take the back part of the Pinto apart to clean up the mess.

I will now share a useful mouse trapping technique. Some mousetraps are scent baited, but I have never found that this works all that well. So here's what I do, I take a small piece of paper towel, and impregnate it with peanut butter. I then cram it into the bait area of the trap as tightly as possible. If you just use peanut butter, the little monster will just lick out the peanut butter. If you plan to use the trap out of doors, drill a hole in it and use a piece of string to tie it to something. As I used this technique a lot when I was homeless, I felt that it was worth describing here. (I don't care for poison. It pollutes the environment, and the Dead animal is usually in some inaccessible location. Who wants to live with a Dead mouse? Not I.)

After the retreat, I hung out in various locations until I could go back to the Monty campground, including a KOA campground. (I needed a bath.)

Oh, You are wondering where the money is coming

from? When I was living with my father, I fixed and sold lawn mowers, and roto-tillers. I did not do service work, as I had found that I couldn't deal with the customers well. (I used to be an auto mechanic, years before.) I just bought, or was given, old machines, and made what I could of them. The money from this lasted until June of 1992. One thing I had learned about myself was that I could work alone, long term.

From The campground I went to see my father, and new stepmother, in Lebanon Oregon. The reason my father had sold the house, and moved in with his new wife, was that they couldn't afford two houses. I had told them to send my mail to Grants Pass, but they didn't get the message in time, so I had to run all the way back to Madras to pick it up.

I have now gotten to the next stage in my PLAN, Grants Pass, Oregon.

From Madras I drove to Grants Pass, arriving in the late evening. The next morning I got up, and drove toward town, on the freeway. I found a wide place between the first and second interchanges. (There is about three miles between them.) Then I unloaded my camping gear, food and other items. I hid them in the brush above the freeway. I got back in the car and found a storage lot, and stored the car.

Then I walked back to the stuff I had stashed, and packed it up the hill to a spot I had selected. I had to avoid poison oak, and I had to make several trips. It's August, and it's getting warm! Setting up a pup tent is pretty mundane, but it always seems that they put the rocks right where you want to put the pegs! The pup tent I had went with me all through my homeless period. It would keep out bugs, and would give you some privacy, but it was about as water proof as a sieve.

I can't remember exactly what came next. I kept a log of all my activities, but the earliest entry is from August 4, 1990. The earlier ones got pitched when I cleaned out the storage unit I had rented, some time later. I think I went back down to the freeway and checked out the onramps for hitchhikers. I don't recall whether I found any or not.

I will start at the August forth entry in my logbook. I

got up at 5:45 AM, and I went to the upper end for breakfast. (I Know I had breakfast at the Golden Arches at least once.) Then I went back to the Cloverleaf area near the freeway, and waited for the sprinklers to come on. This is one way to clean up, and cool off. The people driving by on the freeway must have thought I was nuts. I did wear cut offs. I gave a gospel tract to a hitchhiker, and took a bath in a sprinkler. Then I went to the Laundromat, to wash clothes. I walked to West End, and met two hitchhikers, to whom I gave tracts. I walked back to the East End to the tent. It was very hot. (I remember buying one of those super large soft drinks at a service station. It didn't last long, but it was very refreshing.) As I recall it was 104 degrees.

This I my service to the Lord Jesus Christ, The hitchhikers and the homeless people. I used to hitchhike too, and talk to the people who picked me up, but I got too old. (Nobody would pick me up.) I started doing this after the Lord got a hold of me in 1970. I've written a book about that as well.

Sunday, August five, I walked to the West End, and left material under The freeway overpasses. (Hitchhiker traps.) I talked to three hitchers, and gave out one tract. I spent all day waiting, and watching. Somewhere along the line I talked to a service station attendant. I was always concerned that I should come down with AIDS, or something else, when checking under overpasses, but I never did.

Monday, August sixth, up at 5:30 AM, break camp, pick up car; pick up Camp gear, etc. I talked to one hitcher before I left, and one more en route. I stopped in an area called Rice Valley, north of Grants Pass, and rested. I was there for two nights, in an area that had seen some logging. I drove the car through some tall grasses, which were higher than the car, to get out of sight. It's a wonder that I didn't hit something solid. I had to clean the weeds out of the radiator

After my rest cure, I went north to Eugene, and spent the day in Armatage Park. I was trying to get a hold of some friends I had made, back in the 70s when I was hitching. In the process I ran into some people who were moving. One of their vehicles had electrical problems, so I dusted off my mechanical skills, and fixed it. I spent the night in a rest area further north. I didn't get my friends on the phone for over a year, but if I hadn't been there those people could have been stuck. I like to think the Lord had something to do with me being there.

On to Salem! I stayed two nights in the KOA campground, just south of Salem Oregon. It's right next to the freeway, and, with a handy hole in the fence that someone had made, I could get right out and go to work. I was still in the rest mode, so I didn't do anything that day. Waiting and hanging around and trying to be inconspicuous is wearying, at least to me. Might explain why homeless people always seem lazy. It's about like waiting for a plane, only all the time.

The next day I've got some zip, and I walked north to Market Street. I handed out six tracts to the litter patrol. One of the gals on the litter patrol said she was a Christian. I told her to read it, and if she saw fit, find someone to give it to. I passed one to a hitcher as well. Then I went back to camp. I talked to one of the staff at the campground about spiritual things. When I say I talked to somebody, that usually means some kind of spiritual discussion. I don't preach, there is a back and forth communication between two or more parties.

The next morning I went to The Dalles, Oregon, and set more hitchhiker traps. I spent the night near Lyle, Washington, and rested Sunday. There was some forest fires in the area, so I watched the airplane scoop up water to drop on the fire.

Monday found me checking on my Grandmother, and Uncle. Both now deceased, but both were very much alive then.

The Pinto was giving me trouble, the throw out bearing in the clutch was making a noise. I had changed it before, but there it was again. I spent the night in the Cascade Locks KOA, and tried to figure out what to do. Then I remembered some old friends. (If you read this you'll know who you are, Thanks again.) They weren't at home, but their son was. He let me use their garage, and in about four hours I changed the throw out bearing. In the process I

5

discovered that the front u-joint was bad as well, and fixed that too.

In thanks I took the young man out to dinner. My log says much discussion, but as most of it was about his personal business, and the counsel I gave him, I can't say more. I hoped I helped. (He was about 22 at that time.)

Now for the next part of my PLAN, but first I have to wait for everything to come together. So while I'm waiting I use the time to, put out tracts, and visit my Sister. (Who lived in Forest Grove.) I went out to Cannon Beach Conference and fixed their lawn mower. I rested on the Washington side of the Columbia River, near Cathlamet.

Now I've got to try to figure out what's eating on the car. It's not running right. It's a good thing I'm a mechanic, or I would have been walking a lot sooner than I was! It turned out that the distributor shaft was wobbling. Well it would run, so I drove it to Gresham, Oregon, and ordered a new one.

When I got the new one it wouldn't run!?! I found a loose connection, and now it would run, but it was worse than it was before I bought the new distributor! Here I am, running around Portland, Oregon, in a car that sputters more than it runs. I managed to get it over to where they are going to dock the boat. The boat, well that's the next part of the PLAN. In the process of driving the car over to the dock, I discovered what the problem with the car was. I had purchased a new distributor cap to go along with the new distributor. I discovered, upon inspection, that when they had manufactured the distributor cap, they had left out the center carbon. I took it back, and they gave me a new one. No more problem.

Canvasback Missions is a nondenominational Christian organization, set up to minister to medical needs in the Countries that were formed from the old Trust Territories of the Pacific area. At this time, they were going to the Republic of the Marshal Islands. They had a 72-foot sailing catamaran called the Canvasback, which they use to go to these out-of-the-way Islands. Most of them are Seventh Day Adventists, which I most definitely am not! (I think it's time I described my beliefs, which are basically Baptist, although

6

not a member of any congregation. I call myself a Jesus Person, as I came out of the Jesus movement of the seventies.) There is, however, enough similarity of belief, and purpose, for me to help them. (They do not name their children on those Islands until they are a year old, because most of them don't live that long. I can hope that the situation is improving.)

To understand how I got to know these people, I have to go back to the fall of 1985. I found myself at loose ends, and went out to Cannon Beach. (I can't remember all the details.) I was referred to a man I will call "J," (That's as much of his name as you are going to get.) who knew some people that were building a sailboat to do medical missionary work. They wanted volunteers to help build it.

So, not having anything else to do, and wanting to serve the Lord, I volunteered. They provided room and board, and lots of interesting work. I've always liked jigsaw puzzles; here I got to make my own pieces! (To the design, of course!)

They didn't quite know what to make of me, after all Christians are respectable. (They don't hang out.) After a while they realized that I came to work, and I had, by the Grace of God, some ability.

After a few weeks they made me the director of mechanical installations. My job was to prepare the hulls for the; engines, rudders, and propeller shafts. I also did deck layout, as I knew how to sail, and rig lines so they wouldn't foul one another. I also fabricated, and installed the bilge piping system.

They were nice people, and I was sorry to leave, but after about four months I had had it. (I didn't know of my limited emotional capacity then.) In the summer of 1986 I had helped launch the boat, and had done some work fitting it out afterward. So when I showed up and wanted to help with the haul out they were happy to have me.

The location they used to haul the Canvasback out at, was the Swan Island docks, on the Willamette River side. When I drove up to the guard shack at the gate, the man said, "You can't come in." Then I told him, "but I've got the pullers to pull the propellers!" (Which I did.) I always seem to have a lot of tools around. So they let me in.

When they pull a boat like this out of the water, they position huge nylon straps under the boat in exactly the right spots. If they don't do this right they can break the boat. Then they lift it out using a traveling dock crane, of about 60 tons capacity. (The boat displaced (weighed) 13 metric tons.) The fun is not over yet. Now that we have it up in the air, we now have to set it down! To set it on they have four concrete blocks, about 4'x2'x3'. Once again we have to set it down just so. Here I am with this piece of 2"x4", the boat is swinging around, someone else is trying to steady it, (Several someone else's.) there are three other people, one each to the block, and ain't this fun. We got it down all right. PTL!

I thought that the above episode might prove interesting, or even amusing, which is why I described it.

The rest of the Job was not routine, but I will not bore you with a blow by blow description. We had much to do, and our time on the dock was limited to three weeks. I was the anchor watch, which means I slept aboard to keep an eye on things. I also checked for tools that had been left out from the day's work. They had security here, but they weren't around all the time.

I was involved with the propellers, drive shafts, and propeller shaft brakes. (We had to make the propeller shaft brakes from scratch.) The staff of the machine shops, metal fabrication shops, and welding shops, volunteered their help, without which we wouldn't have finished in time. I was also involved in repairing, And adjusting the out board motors, sanding and painting the hull, and alnodizing the floor of the main cabin. The boat was made of high silica formula, (6061?) aluminum. This formula is almost impervious to corrosion in salt water, but someone had carelessly left some bronze fittings under the floor of the wheelhouse, which, in my opinion, caused the corrosion that we found there. That is why we had to alnodize under the floor of the main cabin.

8

We got the boat back in the water OK. Then I went to Cannon Beach, to drop off a book. I went back to the Corvallis area, saw my father, and some friends, and built the top carrier for the Pinto. This brings me to the next stage of the PLAN.

Chapter Two

I had talked to a travel agency about the trip I wanted to make, so now I went back to buy the tickets. The tickets had to be confirmed about 48 hours before the flight, so I had to do this en route. I drove to Los Angeles, and found a storage lot for the car, and across the street a self-storage operation. After parking my worldly goods, I pushed my cart to the LAX airport. It was several miles, but as I was broken into walking, there was no problem. I had to go a round-about route, as there was an expressway in my path.

My father had built a box for the back of a motorcycle That I had had, and with some parts from the small engine work I used to do, I had built a cart. I knew that I was going to make this trip, so I built it before I left my father's old place. I took two 8"-ball bearing wheels, and made a framework that mounted on the box, with the wheels at the bottom of the box. It had a handle, and looked like a hand truck. I had designed it so you could take it apart with a nut driver, and put all the parts in the box. It flew as luggage. I had installed eyebolts in the box so I could strap my luggage to it. It saved me some money, as I didn't have to rent any of those carts at the airports.

When I got to the airport, I needed a bath, so I rented the facilities in the international section of the airport. I can't remember whether I checked in first or not, but after doing the bath, and checking in, I went to my gate. I had quite a wait, so I amused myself people watching. I also spoke to others who were waiting, but not about spiritual things. Some time in the early evening, my flight was called, and I was on my way.

I arrived late a night in Honolulu Airport, Hawaii. I spent the next two days there, in the airport. It seems I been a little too punctual. (I always like to give myself some leeway in a time schedule situation.) The flight I was waiting for was in the early hours of the morning. There was a large group of people waiting, but as I had gotten there early I got through soon. I just dropped my passport on the desk and tickets, a quick look from the official, and I'm on my way. Amazing what a homeless person can do!

While I was waiting I talked to a Senator from one of the Island republics further west. He was a Christian, but his Bible had some books missing, and parts of others. Seem the missionaries had not, for some reason, completed the work. The Bible is a book on how to live the Christian life. Leave something out of it, and it's like leaving something out of your life. (Even more than that, maybe like leaving something out of God's life?) Not too cool.

We, that is the people on the plane and I, took off more or less as scheduled, and landed on several islands en route to my first destination, the island of Kosrai. I arrived so lagged from all the traveling, that the Immigration people couldn't read my handwriting. (Never very good at best.) I had filled out the papers on the plane, but no good. They weren't too happy, but they finally filled them out for me. I would here like to thank them for their forbearance, not to mention patience.

One of the officials at the airport had a hotel, and I rented a room from him. It was called the Kosrai hotel, and had three other rooms upstairs besides mine. It had an outside stair case, so I never learned what it was like down stairs, besides the office. It was very clean, and they had all the usual amenities, two double beds, shower, refrigerator, (Pop, no alcohol, I don't drink anyway.) air conditioning, and there was no TV. They had bananas by the bunch, eat all you want. No kidding, a four foot stick of them hanging on the wall on the veranda. You really could go bananas in a place like this! They also had small lizards that ran around on the walls. (To eat the bugs?) They had some Kosraian tangerines. These deserve description, so here it is, they were green, sweet, with a lemony taste. Yummy! I only got a couple of them, but they were sure great eating.

I had gone there to see what the spiritual needs of the place were. So I asked the staff of the hotel where the local pastors could be found. They referred me to one pastor who was close to the hotel, and two others at some distance. I went to see the close one first, he asked me questions about my beliefs, and, as I recall, told me I should talk to the head pastor of the island.

The people at the hotel said they could provide transportation, I asked if I could get a ride. The driver had to get ready, and then we were off, at the fantastic speed of 40 kph. (About 25 mph.) That was the island speed limit. The main roads are paved. Some of the vehicles came from Australia, so the steering was on the wrong side, for the right side of the road. I drove this one later when the driver was unavailable, weird!

I was to learn that these people won't let you walk. Just try it, someone would come along and stop and ask, "do you want a ride?" I would always accept, as I didn't want to abuse their hospitality. Coming from a country where hitchhikers can wait for hours before getting a ride, this came as quite a surprise.

One of the pastors I met didn't speak English, but seemed a man of excellent spirit. I'm looking forward to talking to him in heaven, one day, I always tried to speak a more basic English than we speak in the USA. No point in confusing these people with all our colloquialisms.

The next pastor I met was the head pastor of the island. I'll call him pastor "S." When I told him why I had come; he shared with me a problem that they having with one of their pastors. I grieved with him that a pastor could have done such a thing. (I'm not going to describe what.) Then I related a somewhat similar, but different situation, in which the pastors had quit. Pastor "S" said, "If he would do that there would be no problem." Then I said, "The scriptures tell us what to do in such a situation, but the problem is the relationships."

I had offered him some Bibles that I had brought with me. He invited me to speak to his fellow pastors at a meeting they were going to have in a few days, to settle this problem pastor thing. I was NOT to speak about the pastoral situation. That, very properly, was their Job! I was just to talk about the Bibles.

The next day I went to the Post Office to make changes to my schedule. I could see that these people didn't need much help, so there was no reason to stay as long as I had planned. I was certain the Lord wanted me to go there, but it would be many months before I knew why. (At least as far as I could know to date.) The Post Office building housed the offices of the airline. It was an U.S. Post Office, but they had their own stamps. Those islands used U. S. money as well.

I had decided to walk to the Post Office, but in the process I was picked up by, (You guessed It.) a pickup. The front was full, but they had room for me in the back, so away we went. They said that they were going to the Post Office, but would make a stop or two on the way. We turned of on a side road, and then into someone's drive area. We were there for several minutes. While we were there, an old man handed me a pancake and said, "eat cake." So I thanked him and ate cake.

The extreme poverty of these people can not be over emphasized. Yet they shared their food, fruit, and rides with me, a total stranger from a foreign land. On food stamps and camped in the woods, I was better off than most of them. The only advantage they had is no taxes. It's a good thing too, because most of them couldn't have paid them. Someone in one of the rides I was given, gave me some oranges, as well.

As we were leaving, I noticed a toddler wandering near the road. A little girl only a year or two older, wrapped her arms around her little friend, (Or brother?) and pulled him out of harms way. I will never forget the way that child's face beamed. She had helped, and it was good. I will contrast that with this; when I was in the third grade, I was pushed in front of a car, which hit me and knocked me down. One of the kids from school did it. I was not injured.

When I was at the Post Office, I bought some food at one of their stores. Their stores come in two sizes, convenience and about the size of a firework stand. They open them when they please, and close them when they please. There was a man from Finland at the hotel. He was doing economic development work there, under the auspices of the United Nations. We talked a lot, but not about spiritual things. The islander's flexibility in their schedules was driving him crazy, but it gave them time with their kids.

I went to the airport to make a phone call, and on the way back I was picked up by a man I will call Mr. "S." (Not the same as pastor S.) We were both the same age, and we got to talking. It seems he was a Deacon in the local Church, and was the Port Director for the island.

He asked me if I would be interested in seeing some ruins on his island. I was very interested, so I said, "Thanks, Yes." (I'm a frustrated archaeologist somewhere inside.) Then we went to Lealu, the largest town on the island, where the ruins were.

On the way he showed me the sleeping woman, which is a rock formation, high above the town of Lealu. You could see the profile of a woman from her head to below her chest. She was green; the entire island was green. They have about 200 inches of rainfall a year. (Sometimes Kosrai has been referred to as the Island of the sleeping woman.)

When we got to the ruins, I saw a stone wall, made of huge rocks. There was a gap in the wall where a stone, about six feet long and eighteen inches in the center, narrowing to about six inches at the ends, had fallen from the wall.

He was very excited, and filled with wonder. He exclaimed, "do you see that big rock?" "How did they get that rock up there?" The wall was about sixteen feet high. (I'm not at all sure of how tall it was; it might have been more like twelve feet high.) I didn't tell him, that with some stout poles and a half dozen strong men, I could put his rock back where it came from, and not take very long about it either. He was a really nice fellow, but bootstrap engineering was not his field.

On the way back he told me of his grandfather, who had been King of the island. It seems he was walking with his grandfather when he was a little boy. A woman had run up and tried to do obeisance to the old man. The ex-king

14

said to her, "That's all over now, go on about your business." The King had, on his own, abolished the monarchy and the nobility. I told Mr. "S," "He must have been a man of tremendous character to do that."

The next day was Sunday, so I went to Church, morning and evening. They had me sitting with the Deacons and Elders. The Deacons have a higher rank in their church than the Elders do. Someone gave me a breadfruit fan, as there was no air conditioning. The temperature ran between 70 and 90 degrees, the humidity was between 70 and 90 percent. Talk about sauna, and with all those people in there! There was no room for all of them to sit in pews, so some of them sat on the floor. They were working on a new sanctuary, so that problem was being fixed.

The people were segregated as to sex; the men sat on the right side of the church, and the women on the left. I didn't understand the language, but Pastor "S" told me the text was from Amos, chapter 7, the plumb line. He asked me if I wanted to speak, but as I had not prepared, I declined, with thanks.

The singing was done a cappella, (Without instrument accompaniment.) with both sexes singing multiple parts. One elderly lady acted as a pitch pipe, and gave the key. I learned to appreciate this kind of music when I was in a cappella choir in High School. They were very good, and were a joy to listen to, too bad I didn't understand the words. I understand that a choir from there had sung outside the island, whether the music has been recorded or not I don't know.

While I was at Church a Mr. "J" said that he would like to see me. He was the Cultural Director for the State of Kosrai. He told me of the museum, which I saw the next day.

Monday was fairly busy. I started walking to Lealu, but as usual, they wouldn't let me walk, and so I wound up in the back of a pickup. A man that was riding in the back gave me a coconut, for which I thanked him. (He didn't speak any English, but seemed glad to do it.)

On to the museum. It was quite interesting, but not very big. I saw a picture of Mr. "S's" grandfather, the king. There was a history of the kingdom, with the missionary works, and all. The Missionaries had had a bad time trying to convert the islanders, but had finally gotten it done.

The harbor at Lealu had been a haven for pirates, at one time. There was supposed to be buried treasure here somewhere. Where? As with most treasures, it either never was, or was dug up and spent long ago.

On to the State Offices, which were located near the Post Office. Mr. "J" and I had an interesting discussion, but not, as I recall, about spiritual things. Then back to Lealu for the meeting.

I had to wait for the meeting, as it was in the mid-afternoon. While I was waiting, I drank, (Yes, drank.) the coconut the man had given me. The coconut that we get in the states is just a poor relation to the fruit that man gave me. It was very refreshing. I also looked at my first, and probably last, mangrove swamp.

I arrived at the scheduled location, with reasonable punctuality. Pastor "S" made the introductions, and told the other pastors that I had something to say. I then began my speech, it went something like this, "I would like to see that you get some Bibles." "I have heard that there is a shortage here, and could see that you get some." "They would be English Bibles though, and that might be a problem for you."

They talked it over, and came to the conclusion that Kosraian Language Bibles would better serve their purpose. They apparently had a source, but they would have to order them in quantity, to get a discount. They weren't too happy with the sales representative. Seems that a woman in that position, treating with men as an equal, didn't go over very well. (It was a male oriented society.)

Then I had the only time, while I was there, that I had to walk. I didn't really want to either, as my shoes had developed a problem in their soles. I walked quite a ways, and then my Finnish friend from the hotel picked me up. What had happened was the islanders take a nap in the afternoon. Oh well.

Sometime in the later part of my stay on the island, as I was walking back to the hotel, a car stopped beside me. A girl of about nine said, "My Mother (Who was driving.) doesn't speak any English." "Do you want a ride?"

I didn't have far to go, but got in, and expressed my thanks. The little girl said, "No problem." No problem was almost an island motto, as I learned.

When I got back to the hotel, I sat for a while on the upper veranda, and watched the kids playing. They played quietly, no problems, no hassles, and no supervision. I want to point this out, as it will play a large part in some conclusions I made about myself, and the society we live in.

I watched a boy of about nine climb up a breadfruit tree. The tree was a large one, and well picked over. He had to climb into a difficult situation to get one, as there were only a few left. I hoped he wouldn't fall, but he got his prize, and went home.

The next morning I checked out of the hotel. Then I went to the airport, to fly on to the next destination on my schedule. Guess what! The airplane had broken, and I couldn't leave until the next day. I went to the ticket agent and said, "I have a confirmed flight, what am I going to do?" He said, "You are our responsibility." Then he fixed me up with a room in the Coconut Palms Hotel, and a meal ticket in a local restaurant. The meal ticket was good for three meals, but I only used two, because of flight scheduling.

The Port Director, Mr. "S," was of course, at the airport, and he invited me to lunch. He told me, "Order what you want." So I ordered chicken curry. I was very spicy and hot, and was served with rice. Goood! The only problem was there was too much curry. So I asked my host, "do you want some of this curry?" So he went back and got a helping of rice, and baled himself up some curry.

Then he shared an interesting island custom with me, "If two or more people go into a restaurant together, and sit at the same table, and if one of them sees something he wants on someone else's plate, he just reaches out his fork and eats it. (Right off the plate!) "If two or more people go into a restaurant separately, they leave each other's food alone." In that restaurant was the only TV that I saw on the island. They must have been running it off a VCR, as there was no TV station on the island.

Then Mr. "S" and I went back to the airport, and sat in his office and shared testimonies. He had quite a story to tell, but I will not share it with you, as it is his story. A tremendous Christian man.

The next day the plane flew! I want to put in a plug for Continental Airlines, and their daughter company, Continental's Air Micronesia. Their food was good, they put up with the several changes I made in my schedule with good grace, their people were helpful, and when the plane didn't fly, room and meals were provided.

Pastor "S" was on the plane. He gave me some oranges, and helped me get located, when I got to my next destination, Pohnpei.

The reason I was on Pohnpei was the same as in Kosrai, see what the needs were. I already knew of one, because this was the island that the Senator was from, which I had met when I left Hawaii. I never did get together with him, but I tried a lot.

Pohnpei is a totally different situation than Kosrai. For one thing it is the Capital of the Federated States of Micronesia, of which Kosrai is one. For another the population was about forty thousand, over five times what the population of Kosrai. There were two ethnic peoples represented there as well, Micronesians, and some Polynesians. The Polynesians had been relocated there when there had been a famine on their island, in the early twentieth century. The City of Kolonia was where I stayed when I was there. It probably had about half the population of the island living there.

There were two kinds of places to stay on Pohnpei, regretfully I couldn't afford the decent places, and so wound up in a real flophouse. Mattress on the floor, not too clean, and they only turned the water on part of the time because the pipes had holes in them. (Not leaks, holes.) I had a fan in my room, a table and chair, but that was all.

I didn't do all that much while I was in Pohnpei. I walked around, saw the sights, looked at an old Japanese tank they had sitting next to the tourist bureau, looked at what was left of an old Spanish fortress, and read a lot.

I went to Church in an old, tall Church building that sat on a ledge of earth near the port area. The Church service was in English, and was good, old fashioned, basic evangelical Christianity. After the service I talked to the Pastor about some Bibles and pencils I had brought with me. He said they could use them.

When I went through immigration, the officials told me that if I had brought in pens they would have had to charge me duty on them. As it was, no charge. I had some pens back in the States, but something told me not to bring them. (God!) They had another use. The pencils had scripture verses on them, as did the pens.

Then it was time to leave, so I put my cart/luggage together, (The people at the airports thought it was wonderful.) checked out of what passed for a hotel, and headed for the airport.

As I was pushing my cart along, here came a cab. He said he wouldn't charge me anything, he just wanted to give me a ride! I have never heard of a cab driver giving free rides. Only in the islands could such a thing happen. I thanked him profusely.

After I had checked my baggage, I had some time before my flight, so I walked over to see something that aroused my curiosity. Some people had a bunch of small planes and a hanger. It turned out to be a mission organization called Pacific Missionary Aviation. I asked what they did, so one of the missionaries there answered my questions, and told me about their work.

It seems they deliver missionaries, and supplies all over the outer islands. Some of these islands have airstrips, others don't. When they need to get supplies into an island with no airstrip, they parachute them in. They use bed sheets for parachutes. They deliver whatever, and whoever is needed, including medical supplies. (I don't know if they drop people by parachute or not. Those islands are not very big, suppose you land in the lagoon, or worse in the ocean? You could drown, or be eaten, or both.) Then it was plane time, and I'm on my way.

In order to get to Hawaii, you have to cross the International Date Line. So I took off at one PM from Pohnpei on October third, and landed on Hawaii at one AM October third. (That is no misprint.) Those islands were just north of the equator, so I didn't cross that line.

My flight left Honolulu at eight AM the next morning, so I didn't get much rest. Because of time zones, I didn't get back in time to pick up my car or possessions. I pushed my cart to a point near the place where my car and possessions had stored, then camped for the night in the weeds near the freeway. Yes, I know that this is Los Angeles, and that it's dangerous

The next morning I went over to the storage places, and picked up my car, and items. Then I headed for the Mojave Desert. I camped in Nevada, in the extreme southern end of the state. That was the end of my PLAN.

I had hoped that I would find suitable occupation, and some economic security in the course of the last few months activities. I could not have known that it would not work that way for me, and that I must take a longer road. It was time to make a new plan.

Chapter Three

I couldn't stay in the location where I was, as I had to check the mail. I stashed my homemade car top carrier, and loaded it with some of my possessions. Then I drove to Bullhead City, Arizona where I checked the mail; I found some cheap jeans, and tried to get in touch with a brother in Christ. He was doing some work in the direction I had chosen to go. I say tried, because I didn't succeed. I was still lagged from the plane trip, but decided to go on anyway. By this time it's late in the evening.

I drove all night, arriving in Fort Stockton, Texas, the next day. My log says that I talked to four hitchers en route. I rented a spot to park in the KOA camp ground, for three days. I was still trying to get over being jet lagged.

On to Corpus Christi, Texas. I was very concerned about the lack of regular gas. They were phasing out leaded fuels, and that's what my car needed to run on. The unleaded gas ran a lot hotter, and I was concerned that the car should burn a valve or a piston. (Never happened.)

As I have done in the past when hunting a job, I checked the places where someone might have heard of something. I was looking for another Canvasback project. I met a brother who had a garage full of Christian books, and checked on a Christian farm. Nothing was happening there, so I worked my way up the gulf coast. I parked for the night between Fulton, and Tivoli, Texas. More checking the next day, and the day after that.

Somewhere along there I must have started sounding discouraged. A man, (Brother in Christ?) encouraged me to keep on. I don't remember what he said, but it helped.

I had bought an interesting book when I was in the islands. When I got to Palacious, Texas, I sent it to a friend in Oregon. Then I went to Victoria, Texas to a used bookstore there. I was always finding books in the used book-

21

stores.

I took several days off, then went through Galveston, to the Baytown KOA. Baytown is just East of Houston, Texas. I arrived with perfect timing, as a hitcher and myself got there at the same time!

I still had some idea of a boat ministry, so I went boat shopping. I knew the Lord could provide, so why didn't He? I couldn't think that there was something wrong with me. I didn't have a clue.

I met a man as I was going to dinner, and he told me about his fellowship group. Remember the pens that I didn't take to the Islands? When I would eat in restaurants, I would leave one of the pens with the message on it, on the table as I left. (I was not very happy about eating in restaurants, as my money was fading fast. I see now that this was one was of spreading the Word.)

After a few days there, I went back to Corpus Christi, and then to Mustang Island. I would spend the next two weeks there. My activities were, walking on the beach, checking the mail, and talking to people, reading, and making plans. (No use in the plans I made, but how was I to know.) I changed my location several times during this period.

I went to Corpus Christi to check on things, then on to park on Saint Jo Island. I spent the next several days there. The next day after I started parking on Saint Jo Island, I went to Corpus Christi to check on this and that. When I went to go through an intersection, the engine just quit. The Pintos had a toothed belt to run the camshaft, and distributor. This had stripped off some of its teeth. I had just enough momentum to coast to a parking area where I could work on it. I took off the old belt to use as a sample, and walked very fast to a parts house that was about two miles away. I bought the belt, and made the round trip in about an hour, more or less. I wanted to get the car fixed before someone told me to have it towed.

When the owner of the house I was parked in front of came home, he asked me, "Does your car run?" I could answer, "It does now." I had got it running, and made some adjustments. All I had to do was put on the timing cover, and put away my tools, when he showed up. I finished those tasks and left. PTL!

The end of October found me back on the beach. I went for a walk on the beach on November first, and found a can of WD-40. There wasn't too much in the can, but the stuff comes in handy so I kept it.

I moved to a location down the road to the bay side of the island. While I was there I baled out an old boat, to see if it could be fixed. (No way.) The prickly pear cactus in the area had some ripe pears on them. I tried one, it was very peppery, and it stained my mouth and teeth purple. (Only temporary, thank God!)

I saw this truck traveling along the highway in the distance. The sign on the side said, "Lack's Furniture." I don't see how. Later when I was in Portland, Texas, I saw that they had a whole showroom full! Dumb huh?

On November fifth I started staying near Kennedy Causeway. You could stay one night, and then you had to get permission from the parks department. You could only stay a few days, but it was nice to camp legally. The other places were only legal if no one complained. I moved around often enough that no one got the idea that I was going to put down roots.

While I was at the causeway, I met a man by the name of Scott. He was hitching to California, and was waiting out a storm. He had taken shelter under the over-hang of the causeway. We had quite a long talk, and he gave me a book to read, so I gave him one of mine. I hope I did him some good.

Over the next two and a half weeks I hung out, moved around, put out pens and tracts, picked up various items as I walked, and did a lot of reading. I was walking more and more as an economy measure. I finally wound up near a river near Mud Bridge Rd. (The name fits.) The area I was in was OK, but the way there was mud city. I finally pried the dried mud out from under the car in Arizona.

Soon after I got there, the Police checked me out, but they didn't ask me to leave. PTL! I was searching for a place to relieve myself, in the dark with a flashlight, when I noticed something in the weeds. It was a scissors jack. It was lacking in lubrication, so someone had pitched it. I oiled it up and it worked fine. I also found some other things, mostly tools, as I was walking around.

Amazing how people can be so careless with something as useful as tools. My father, when I was a child, gave me some old and clumsy tools, and an old ammo box to put them in. I left them out in the rain, and was chastised for my carelessness. Good training.

On Thanksgiving Day I was hanging around the area, waiting for I knew not what. Two young men were looking around, and stopped their pickup near me. I think they wanted to fish in the river, but didn't like where they were at, and so tried to start their pickup, and failed. I went over to see what was wrong, and lo and behold, sparks were jumping around inside their distributor cap. I took it off to see what was wrong, and saw all these black marks inside it. There was also some condensation in the distributor cap. I went back to my car and got the can of WD-40 that I found on the beach, and squirted some inside. I put the cap back on, and told them to start it, and it took right off. I told them that this was only a temporary fix, and it might not run again after it was shut off. I also told them how to fix it. They were very thankful and gave me a basket of nuts. So we all had something to be thankful for on Thanksgiving Day.

It was becoming obvious that I was not getting anywhere here, so I made arrangements to have my mail stopped, and was on my way again. On November 27, late in the day, I had all my arrangements made. I drove to a rest area about forty miles west of San Antonio, Texas. The next day I was on the road again. I drove all that day, and the next night as well. I arrived at a point between Parker, and Quartzite, Arizona, early the next morning. I had a short nap, and went for a walk on the highway. My, my, those careless people. My log says that I found straps, a mirror, and tools. The road was very rough there, and I suppose the stuff

24

shook off.

For the next week I wandered around, hiking up the roads, and picking up loads of things to sell in the swap meets. Then I went to an old friend of mine's place. He was not a Christian, but we shared some of the same interests. I got there on Friday, late, and we spent the weekend together. He had some interesting documentaries on tape, and we went hiking. We also visited some of his co-workers. I have talked to him about spiritual things for twenty-five years. I am still in contact as I write this. I can only pray that someday this will have a positive effect. (I lost contact with him in 2001.)

From there I went to see if the things I left, when I went to Texas were still there. They were, so I loaded some of them up. The next month or so I spent in the Mojave Desert. I was hiking around, selling in the swap meet, (I didn't even break even.) being very cold, and just plain surviving.

The next step is to go to a camper conference that is held in Indio California. I rented a motel room, and morning and evening, I walked to the conference. What a break from the nomad life. I was respectable again! Unfortunately it was only temporary.

I got a lot out of the discussions, met some nice people, shopped around, and got a hair cut. The Desert Storm war started while I was there, so I watched the news on the TV at the motel. The conference was selling cheap Bibles, so I bought one. I've still got it, but it's falling apart. I finally bought another to replace it with after it had served me for years.

From Indio I went to the Bouse, Arizona spectator area, near the off road racecourse. They were about to have the race, and I waited for that event.

The racers pre run the racecourse to familiarize themselves with it, and so run the race faster. I was sitting there, watching, when around the corner came a pre runner, extremely fast. He (They) was already sideways to the road when I saw them. The four-wheel drive rig immediately turned over, and over, and part way over. I ran down, it was a hundred yards or more, and peered inside. "Are you guys all right in there?" I asked. They assured me that they were all right, but their suburban wasn't!

They climbed out the back, and surveyed the damage. It was laying on it's side, and they wanted me to turn it over, using the Pinto. I was having clutch trouble, and told them no way. Awhile later someone came along with a better rig, and got them turned over. They were well strapped in, or they could have been seriously injured, or even killed.

One of the race officials was by a day or so later. He was putting up signs telling people that the road would be closed on race day, and for a day or so before. I went down to where he was working, and asked if I could help on race day. He indicated there was a possibility, so we left it at that.

Two days later, here came a motor home. The people in it told me that I was a Score Race Official. They told me that they wanted me to man the roadblock, and stop people from going up the road. I was also to report anyone that was driving around, off road, and outside the spectator area. They could walk or ride horses, but no vehicles. They gave me an orange safety vest, and official score vehicle stickers for my car. They gave me a two-way radio later. They told me that there would be some other volunteers to help, as well. How 'bout that!

So I moved my car down near the road block area, collected up a lot of fire wood, and got ready for the traffic. The next day was Friday, during which I helped maintain the roadblock. The Deputy Sheriffs took over at night, which was a big help.

Saturday dawned bright and clear, it was race day! The problem with an off road race is you see so little of it. You stand around for hours, and occasionally a vehicle comes through, but that's about it. There was no wind, and the dust just hung around. (It would be two days before I got the dust out of my nasal passages.) It finally got dark, and then the fun began.

The problem was that with all that dust, even with lights, the racers couldn't see all that well. It was about like fog, only not so damp. We had one racer miss the curve entirely, and go flipping end over end, out through the desert.

I went over to see if anyone was hurt, but he was just shaken up by his side trip. He had broken a shock, but he had a spare, and some of us helped him install it.

Some spectators had built a fire, and the vehicle had come within fifty feet of landing in the fire. I went over and explained that they were in an area that could be hazardous. I think that they had already gotten the idea, because it wasn't long before they left. There was one other accident, but not so serious, before my nights work was done. They finally pulled the plug around eleven PM. I was pooped.

From February the twenty-eighth, to March the twenty-sixth, 1991, I walked the off road race courses, and highways, on both sides of the Colorado River. They had discontinued the races on the California side of the river some time before, but there was still a lot of stuff to be found. Scavenger me, but there was no point in letting good stuff go to waste. Besides all this, I like to walk.

I had moved to a spot where I had camped before, (And since.) and decided to walk to Earp, California. It is a distance of about sixteen miles one way. I made it all right, but was very tired. I rested awhile, then walked to a pay phone to call a friend. We were making plans to go camping together.

On the twenty-sixth of March, I left to go to the Houston, Texas area. En route I passed out tracts to hitchers, several of them. The main reason for going was still the boat ministry. I had not yet gotten the idea that this was not my job. Praise the Lord for his patience with me. I can be thankful that the Lord found a use for all my wanderings. The round trip from and to the Mojave Desert took six days.

Then I rattled around the desert some more, in the process of which I found a drive wrench that fit the scissors jack that I found in Texas, in November.

On April sixth, I went to a swap meet they used to have in Needles, California, in the Claypools Hardware parking lot. (They don't have the swap meet anymore.) The first time I sold there, the day was warm, about 106 degrees. I sold a lot of things that I had been finding all winter. My logbook says $32.70, for which I can be thankful. I sold again the next week, but didn't do so well, $3.75. Some friends showed up while I was at the second swap meet, so I had a nice visit anyway.

On Monday, April fifteenth, I stashed my things at the area where I had stashed them before, near the pointed area of Nevada. From there I went to see my friend in Laughlin, Nevada, and spent the night. From my friend's place, I went to explore the area north of Williams, Arizona. I wandered around the area, in the process of which I found a pair of insulated gloves. They came in very handy in a later stage in my life. My friends from Laughlin joined me for a weekend. We explored the south rim of the Grand Canyon, and camped out in the woods together.

My father and his new wife had split up, and he had been very sick, but was better. He said that he would sell the contract on the house he had sold, and buy a motor home. The two of us could live on the Mojave Desert, in the motor home. He wanted to live in a dryer climate, because he was always coming down with pneumonia. He had put some money down on a motor home, and was living in it, please come up. He wanted me to drive the motor home.

I still had the stuff stashed in Nevada, so I left it, and went to Oregon. I drove for two nights, and one day. I arrived, very tired, where my father was staying, near Lebanon, Oregon.

When I got there I found that all was not well. My father was a near invalid from his bout with pneumonia. He had put some money down on the motor home, thinking that he would sell the contract quickly. The motor home that he had chosen had serious structural problems in the body, as well. He was staying with some friends, and living in the motor home.

While I was there, I either camped in my car, (Not a

real good idea in a semi-residential area.) or I stayed in a friend of mine's camper. I either used my car, which was becoming increasingly decrepit, or an old Ford/Mazda pickup that my father owned.

My father and I had a lot of tools between us, so to lighten the load, and eliminate duplication, It was agreed that I would sell my carpenter tools, and my 1/2 drive socket set. This was the start of a mammoth sell off, my father having a lot more things than would fit into a motor home, not to mention my stuff.

The things I had to do to get ready for this lifestyle were these; Fix my father's pickup, and sell things in the yard sales. (My friend with the camper had a barn, which was part of the property which he rented. we used it on a weekend for a barn sale.) I had to sort out the things in the storage unit that my father had rented, and go get things where my father had been living.

Not only that, but the people where my father was living were getting ready to move too. They had an International pickup that needed work, plus they too had things in storage that they wanted to get out. My friends with the camper and the barn needed some help too. I have entries in my log book that mention helping install carpet, work on a twelve HP engine, and just helping on projects. It was the least I could do, as they had been a big help in all this.

In the middle of all this, the company that was looking at my father's contract, decided not to buy it. The broker sent the papers to another company, but that proved to be too long, and the note ran out on the motor home, and they repossessed it.

My father was in a fix, and if it had been winter he probably wouldn't have survived. He had an old, decrepit, and very small travel trailer, which he had been using for storage. It had been gutted of nearly all the amenities, but that is what he had to move into. I will not describe the sanitary arrangements, except to say they were primitive. My father then put some possessions down on another motor home, just to hold it. He never moved into this one, but once again the process took too long, and he didn't get either his possessions or the motor home.

About the end of this period, some brothers in Christ that had decided to start another school like the Ecola Hall School that I had gone to, wanted to have a meeting. They were going to discuss ways and means, and wanted me to come. I stayed with my friends in the Portland area, the ones who had helped me with the clutch, in August of 1990. The next day was the meeting, and afterwards, dinner.

I think they needed more means than ways, as the school never got off the ground. Sometimes you have to go through these things to find out what the Lord's will really is. In other words, it's a learning experience. I've had several of them, and every time I've found myself doing things, and meeting people that I would never have done, or met. This book is an example. You find, after a while, that the Lord has a different purpose than the one you thought.

It was becoming obvious that my father's situation was going to take longer than he originally thought. This meant that I was going to have to do something else with myself, until things came together.

Somewhere in Texas, in the fall of 1990, the car had developed this problem. Push in the clutch, put it in neutral, and it still started in gear. Immediately after it started, the clutch released, and you could drive it normally. (I think that the collar that the throw out bearing rode on, broke.) You had to stand on the brake when you started it, or it could run into things. The first time it did this was quite a surprise! I never did hit anything with it, but did not have either the time or the money to fix it. It had run all this time, but for how much longer? Before I had traded for it, someone had wrecked the filler plug in the rear end, and now the rear end was making a noise. Then the headlight switch went haywire. I was about out of money as well, so I couldn't renew the insurance either.

My father and I had this deal going, and I figured that all I had to do was put myself on hold, and everything would work out. So before I junked the car, I unloaded some stuff at my friend's place, and dropped off the rest, (In the dark.) near a likely camp area.

Chapter Four

Here I am at the wrecking yard. I've got twenty dollars in my hand from the sale of my car. My personal possessions are here and there, my pack is on my back, and I've got about nine miles to walk to my prospective campsite. I am forty-eight years of age. Before I was vehicular homeless, now I'm just plain homeless. It is now June of 1991.

Near my prospective campsite was what used to be a house. There had been a fire, and then the house had been abandoned. It was, by this time, beyond help, as far as repair goes, so I salvaged some boards from it. I did not take them off the property, however. The sad thing about being in a survival situation is that you have to do things that you know are not exactly right, even if you know that no one will complain.

Out of this junk lumber I built an "A" frame construction. It was about seven feet long, six feet wide at the floor, and seven feet high. The floor was of one-inch thick shiplap. The sidewalls only extended a foot or so above the floor, and the end walls were solid, except the east one which had the door in it. I threw a green tarp over this framework, and nailed it down. This was to be my home for the next twenty-six months or so. (Of course, I didn't know this then!)

It was a lot of work getting all this done. I had to pry off the boards I needed, cut then to fit, then pack them through a jungle of blackberries, and other brush. When we had sold off the tools and things, I had sold my handsaw, so now I had to buy another one, which was very dull. I used a piece of wide floor edge molding for a square, which served me in later constructions as well. I had to straighten the nails I needed, and although I remember buying a few, I straightened most of them.

My log says that I got one particular task done just

as it started raining. PTL! (Water is king, and now it's reigning.) The job took about four days of furious work.

While I was doing this, I was also picking up the food and other items that I had earlier stashed in the area. The reason that I was working so hard, I was concerned that it would rain before I was finished. I got done just in time. I would work on finishing up tasks for several weeks, but now I could sleep there.

The principles I had worked out for selecting a campsite were these; It had to be at least 1/2 mile from any residence, good natural concealment, no fires, (I don't smoke either.) a source of building material nearby, outside the city limits, and a access that can't be observed. Water and food I could, and did, pack in.

The idea was to be effectively invisible, not that I was actually invisible, but I wanted to be as inconspicuous as possible. I didn't want people seeing me as I went to and from my camp area.

There are two ways to be unhassled, and be homeless: You can go the grubby route, so that others don't think you have anything, and so leave you alone. This has the disadvantage that none of the rest of the populace wants you around, not to mention the Police. The other way is as I was doing; at least I could take spit baths, and keep myself relatively clean. The Police usually will not hassle you if you are outside the city limits, and no one complains. They have enough to do already.

I applied for food stamps late in June. As I recall, it was at this time that the caseworker suggested that I seek counseling. A few weeks later I went out for water on a Saturday, and ran into a parade. No more weekend trips for water, or much else either. Too conspicuous! I had rented a P.O. box in Philomath, Oregon, and was getting my mail there.

My lifestyle, (If that's what you want to call it?) at this time was one of reading, going to the store for food, or going after water. I never got together with any of the Christian organizations that I wrote to, during this period, for which I now thank God. This kind of work was something that God had not called me to do.

One of the situations that had developed, was that my father had gotten back together with my stepmother. That was the end of the trip south to the desert, and living the mobile lifestyle. My father eventually did get a motor home, which he lived in until they could get married again.

My father's little pickup had motor problems, so we went to a wrecking yard, and bought another motor. Then we towed the pickup to the friend of mine's place that had the barn. I was supposed to change the motor, but some of the bolts were missing, and I couldn't get anyone to get me the bolts I needed to put it together. My father towed the pickup to the wrecking yard, and had them put the engine in. . Neither the installation nor the engine was any good.

What I learned from this was never buy a used engine without hearing it run first. If they've got it sitting on the floor, leave it there! (You can take it apart too.) After I got off the street I bought a used engine from a wrecking yard, and after correcting an oil pressure problem, I've used it for over four years. It was still in the vehicle, and sounded all right, before I bought it.

In mid September I walked west on highway 34, to a point just west of Blodgett. The place I stopped at was a pass in the hills. When they built the road, they made terraces to keep the hill from sliding onto the road. It was quite a scramble to get up on one of these terraces, but once there, it was a great campsite. There were several pine trees growing on the terrace, which gave me good shade, and the needles made for comfortable bedding. In spite of the time of year, it was unseasonably warm, even hot.

Later in the afternoon, I took a walk further up the hill. I found a party balloon that said, "I love you" on it. Inside it was a spider. I think the Lord was trying to tell me something about myself. I was still focused on the boat ministry idea, but now I had the idea that I needed a wife, and that was the hang up. (Wrong again.) There was more to the story than that, but I will not discuss it yet. Once again the Lord was keeping me out of trouble.

33

The next day I walked to a spot about half way between Burnt Woods, and Eddyville. I spent the afternoon picking dead black berry brush out of the place that I had planned to sleep. I walked back to Kings Valley Junction the next day, arriving in the early afternoon. In the process I found a Christian magazine that had an article about asking for a double portion of the Holy Spirit, so I did.

I sat near the road, resting, reading, and watching traffic, all afternoon. At near dark, I crawled under the bridge that was there, to spend the night. It took about two hours the next day to walk back to my campsite.

I had gotten some exercise, learned something of the mind of the Lord, and found a lot of stuff. My food was pork and beans, and peanut butter sandwiches. I may have had a few berries as well. I call this a poor man's vacation.

When I was en route back I found a nice flashlight, with Oregon State Police written on it. So a few days later, I went to the Police office that was located between Corvallis, and Philomath, and returned it. I was told that the Officer that lost it would be glad to get it back, as he was going to be charged the cost of replacing it. I got a nice card from him, thanking me for retuning it.

My friends with the barn had gotten a lot of old lawn mowers, so I walked to their place, a distance of about ten miles, and started setting up a work area in their barn. I was there about a week, and fixed up, ready for sale, three lawn mowers. I also did baby sitting, and helped them cut and stack their winter wood supply. I caught cold, which didn't help me much. It is now October, and cooling off rapidly. I could no longer work in the barn, because there were no lights. I would wait until mid February, when the days were getting longer.

Somewhere along here the Lord seems to have given me something to do in the hitchhiker area, again. (Do this until that happens.) This was in late October.

On the last day in October I got a letter from a friend of mine. He has called a lady that needs someone to handy man work around her place, no money, just board and room.

The situation sounds good, so I call her up, and make arrangements to be picked up on the third of November.

On the second of November the Police arrive, and tell me that I have to leave by the next day. So I hide some of my stuff in the woods, and pack what I need to the appointed place where I was to be picked up. On the third, when I was standing there, the Police Officer that told me to leave drove by. I had told him that I had this deal going, but people lie to the police all the time, so I guess he was checking me out. After a while the lady, and one of the people that lived there, came by and picked me up. The Lord was looking out for me again.

When I was growing up my parents had problems getting along together. So seeing as I wanted to get married as part of my ministry, I thought that I should learn how to deal with the marriage relationship. I had been searching the used bookstores, and junk shops for material on this, with emphasis on the Christian marriage.

I also got books on situations that I was interested in, such as child abuse, as I knew a couple of ladies that had been messed with. I thought that if I, by the will of God, should marry a lady that had been messed with, I would be better equipped to recognize the outworking of such a situation. As there would be no counseling available in the boat situation, I could help with the process of working through the problems inherent in such a situation.

The Bible, in Matthew 7: 3-5, says to take the beam out of your eye, so you can see clearly to take the mote out of your brother's. I didn't have a beam; I had a whole log pile! The only problem was that I didn't know it then. All these books would eventually give me some idea that I had a problem.

Chapter Five

I've really been helped by the Lord, I've got a warm place to spend the winter, food to eat, (I don't even have to cook!) and useful work to do. I have a bunch of books to study, so my spare time should be usefully spent.

The people had several projects on line when I got there, a new water supply system, the electric fence, and the normal odds and ends that go wrong in an older dwelling. The lady took in elderly people, and had in the past taken in foster children. I met several of the former foster children while I was there. She also had some just plain renters, one of which rented the pasture, as well.

After moving in, I had to get my tools, most of which were at my friend's place. Someone took me over to get them. The electric fence was not working, so that was my first project. I had to string wires, and eliminate short circuits. The problem was that the tall grass would short out the wire, especially when wet.

The water supply was a joke, but on who? The screen had holes in it, and as they pumped water out of a creek, they were always picking up mud and other debris. If you took a bath, you didn't know whether you were getting cleaner or dirtier. You'd fill the tub, and couldn't see the bottom! I had to take the pump apart one morning because they had no water. The pump had picked up a small shell, and plugged up.

One time a shell got through the pump, and plugged a pipe, and all they could get was hot (It could have been cold.) water. I figured out where the plug was, but couldn't clear it. I finally came up with an idea. I would use a hose and run it from the spigot that worked to the one that didn't. That would back flush it. I had some help from one of the people that lived there. I was under the house, and had to yell at the person in the kitchen, as to when to turn the water on and off. It worked great, the shell popped right out.

The lady's son was a Police Officer. He was putting in a mobile home, and a new water supply system nearby. The two dwellings would share the new system. They had started on this already, but were far from done. In this project I would assist a man I will call "M." He had a very loud voice, a very sick wife, and some teenagers. He was also a brother in Christ. He was a very handy person, and had the confidence; (justified) of the people I was staying with. We built the pump house over the new cistern, and worked on the new pickup for the water supply.

After I had been there about nine days, I decided to do some work on the project that I felt the Lord wanted me to do. One of the people at the house drove me into town, where I was picked up by my friend with the barn's wife. The next day I went to Albany, Oregon, with my friend, when he went to work.

From there I went to the freeway, (Interstate five) on which I walked south to the highway thirty-four exit. I didn't find any hitchers, but I did find a twenty-five foot tape measure. I already had one, and I didn't know why I needed another. I later sold it, and many other things, to help out my financial situation. PTL!

That night, after we were all in bed, (About 10 PM) Mr. M shows up. Seems they don't want me out there anymore. He has all my things, which he unloads, then and there. I've been staying in my friend's camper, and that's where the stuff will stay for a while.

The lady's Policeman son was concerned for her safety, and that's why I've been evicted. After all I was homeless, and that could be bad. (It didn't feel very good either!)

As I know now, I probably wouldn't have been able to cope with the concentrated social interaction for long. I probably would have split the scene, with all the emotional hassles of sudden separations. I know that I wouldn't have hurt them though. It is not any fun at all to be judged by your situation.

I have several things to be thankful for, and some I've learned from all this. The first is this; When I was staying with these people, I asked the lady how she dealt with foster children. She said, "I raise them just like I raise my own children." This was quite effective, as her son was a Policeman, and her two daughters were a Doctor, and some other professional, respectively.

The problem with this, is just this, children are usually raised the way the parents were raised. This may be modified some but that's the way it's done. This can be very good, or very bad, or somewhere in between. Unfortunately we don't know whether we've done it right until it's too late. It's no good saying it's bad kids, children are what you are, not what you teach them. We just do what feels right, but sometimes this doesn't work too well.

I've got two things to be thankful for; I had a place to go when the Police told me to move, and I had a place to stash my stuff, when the man brought it over in the middle of the night.

The next day I walked to the freeway from my friend's place, then north to Albany. I didn't find any hitchers, and so I came to the conclusion that no one wanted to hitchhike in the late fall, or winter months. I will try again next year in February. That night I went with my friend to Eugene, Oregon. He had some business there, and while there I finally got the people on the phone that I tried to talk to in August of 1990.

After helping my friends with babysitting, and moving lumber for a couple of days, they took me back to the old house where I had salvaged the lumber. (At my request.) I had to reapply for food stamps, because I had stopped them when I move out to the lady's place.

I had lost my insulated gloves, and guess where I found them, upstairs in the old house! I was very thankful. I don't know whether a hunter found them, and left them there, or I forgot and left them.

The reason the police had told me to move was that a hunter had located me there, and complained to the

Police. I have determined to move my camp to another location, but first I have to wait until hunting season is over. For several days I hung out at the old house, then a hunter appears, so I move my things to an old shed in the area. It is very hard to get to, so they should be all right. Then I split for town.

The next week I spent in a shelter, called the Sunflower House, in Corvallis, Oregon. They have counseling, a shelter for abused women, (somewhere, but not there) a men's shelter, a public shower, (I used this at least once a week in the cold months.) and a public kitchen, with dinning area. I used all the above facilities at one time or another, except the women's shelter. (Wrong gender!) They put on a turkey dinner at Thanksgiving, and Christmas. I spent Thanksgiving Day there at this time, and had a good time.

This facility could be used as a model for a camp. You could serve many more people in a camp, than you could in a building.

A day or so before I left, we cleaned house. In the process, I got a lot of dirty sox. They were bad smelling, but otherwise all right. I put them in a plastic bag so they didn't pollute the rest of my stuff. After I washed them, I paired them up, and used them for years. PTL!

On the first of December of '91, I went back to the old area where I used to camp. I then selected a new campsite at some distance from the old one. It was in some black berries, and was difficult to get to, but would provide excellent concealment. I would spend the next twenty-one months there. The only problem with it was, that when it rained hard, there were puddles in the trail and the area of my shelter.

Now I had to move the "A" frame to the new location. It was too heavy to move assembled, so I took it apart. It took me less than two days of work to move and assemble it, then move in. I had good weather all through this period, for which I can be truly thankful.

I had started a Bible study that I call the Keys to the Kingdom. As I read through the Bible, (Three chapters a day.) I would pick out things in certain categories, and make a note of them. They were; common sense, for me to live is Christ, (Phil 1:21) the way, the walk, the work, things to put on, keys to the call of God, and the Kingdom of Heaven. (My concordance was in storage.)

I am not going to give you all my notes, but I am going to give you what I consider to be common sense, as there seems to be so little of it these days.

To learn from your own mistakes, as well as the mistakes of others.

To look at the world as it is, and not how you feel it ought to be, and behave accordingly.

To look for the hand of God, and his will in everything.

To discern the difference between a need and a want.

To realize that what to yourself maybe a need, maybe a want to others, and vise versa.

To be able to see the consequences of a course of action, or attitude, with out having to go through it.

To make sure that people around you have a free choice, and know that there is a choice to be made.

To turn past negative experiences into positive ones, by helping others who have had, or are having, similar experiences. (2 Corinthians 1:4)

To take heed HOW you hear. (Unless we do not want to understand, or to ignore something we don't want to hear, but need to!)

It is well to care about a person, but it is best to know how to care FOR them, and meet their needs.

To the degree a person doesn't care, to that degree they can't be helped.

To care for yourself, is to be able to care for others.

To know that somewhere, someone genuinely cares

for you, will enable you to care for yourself. (In my case, God is that care person.)

In the winter I bundled up, as I had no heat. I would get up in the morning, put my clothes on and eat breakfast. Then I would get back under, but not in, my sleeping bag and blankets. I would read until one hand got to cold, then I would switch hands. On really cold days I would just lay there and survive. I had one of these foam pads with the bumps, but it was too thin.

I had made the mistake of building my bed out of solid plywood. It didn't breathe, or ventilate, so it was always damp. I finally figured out what was wrong, so when I moved out of the area, I made the next bed with slats, with a small gap between them. This worked well. I always built my beds fourteen inches off the floor. This gave me room to stow things under the bed.

At Christmas I went to the Sunflower House for the day. They had to usual feed, plus they gave us all a gift, a pair of sox! They also had a huge box full of things that were supposed to go to Desert Shield, but the war was over too quickly to send. I scored some writing paper, soup, deodorant, sunglasses, and other items. PTL!

One of the things I had to do was make trails. If I kept using the same ones, someone could find me. I needed trails because if I walked through the tall, wet grass, my clothes would get wet. Because I had no heat my clothes took a long time to dry. I'm sure that my clothes didn't last as long as they would otherwise have done if I could have dried them quickly. This was a problem until I got state welfare, in 1994. Then I could afford to buy clothes, when they got too far gone. I knew about thrift stores, but I wear a popular size in pants, and could rarely find what would fit me in a thrift store.

The agency's that provide sleeping bags, and blankets to the homeless, could also take a look at the shoes people need. If the only transportation you have is your feet, you need good shoes to walk any distance at all. Otherwise you can't get to where you need to go to get the services you need, and may get messed up in your survival situation.

The Lord did provide what I needed so that I didn't look too bad, and I always had what I needed in footwear.

On January 24, 1992, I went to a thrift store called ARC, (Americans for Retarded Citizens) to do some shopping. While I was there, I observed some of the staff trying to saw some file carriers with a hacksaw. They were making a very hard job of it, so I asked if I could help. They were happy to let me do it, and it didn't take very long, either. (If you want to cut thin metal with a hacksaw, you need to hold the saw at an angle of forty-five degrees or so, to the work. If you don't you can break the saw blade, and possibly injure yourself. You can also have a lot of trouble starting the cut. A fine toothed blade helps too.) This was the beginning of my work as a volunteer at the ARC thrift store.

Like the Canvasback people, they didn't know what to make of me, as this organization was almost exclusively of women. They were also afraid that I might terrorize them, or something. (They told me about this later.) Once again all I had to do to prove myself was work, and present a reasonable demeanor. As time wore on I found myself in charge of the electrical, and electronics department. My duties were; to check out donated items, clean those that could be resold, and price them out. I usually came in on Thursday, but when I had something else to do on that day, I would come in on Wednesday. I did this until I left the area, in August of 1993.

I was having trouble with my stomach; it seems that I was hitting the books to hard. Apparently the emotional content of the human behavior books I was reading was causing my stomach problem. I didn't want to have an ulcer, so I decided to pace myself. I would read one book every three weeks. No more problem. I would continue this regimen of study, with exceptions for special books, or special studies, all the time I was on the street.

I called my barn friends on the thirteenth of February, only to find out that their marriage was breaking up. I know the hassles it caused me when my folks broke up. This hurts! I knew them fairly well, and I knew that this could happen, but it's still a shock when it does. This was one of the reasons I did babysitting for them. I was hoping that this would give them some time together and work things out. I guess, now, that I must have bonded with them, or something.

They had both told me of the bad things that had happened in their growing up years. Although I tried to counsel with them, I still had this beam in my eye, and so I couldn't see clearly enough to help them. Their problems were such that, except for the Grace of God, either one of them would probably have caused their breakup.

I went over there a few days later, and talked to the husband. (The wife and kids had split.) I had three things to do when I got there, work on the lawn mowers, hike the freeway looking for hitchhikers, and try to settle the husband down. He was so distracted he couldn't even eat. He wanted her back, but as far as I know, that didn't happen.

He went to work in the morning of the eighteenth of February, and I went for a walk on the freeway again. We met at his place of employment. When we got back that evening the neighbors told us that the county Sheriff's Deputy had been there. We immediately assumed that he was going to be evicted. We grabbed all the equipment from his private shop, the vehicles and the camper, and took them to his parent's home.

He thought, I think, that he was going to have to live in the camper, so he wanted my stuff out. I called another friend, who came over, and picked up my stuff and me. We went to his place, where I spent the night. This was the friend that made the arrangements for the handyman job. My things would remain in his attic for over two years. All the county Sheriff wanted to do was serve a restraining order. The Husband went over to the County Court House and picked it up the next day.

With the old food stamps, when you didn't have the money come out even, you got the difference in change. After a while the change would accumulate, so I would roll it up into rolls. Then I would take it to the bank, and exchange it for paper money. It took quite some time to make this worth while. I went to the bank to do this, and after I left the bank, I checked my pocket, and my wallet was gone! So I went back to the bank, and they had my wallet. The Mr. M that I worked with at the lady's place, had found it and turned it in at the bank. All my money and ID were still in it. When I saw him again I thanked him profusely. It seems that he recognized my name from the ID in the wallet, and told the people at the bank to expect me. PTL!

I had to pack water in all the time. During the winter months they turned the water off in the park, so I had to get it at a friend's place, near were I used to live in Corvallis. This was a distance of about eight miles, round trip. I have notes in my logbook that show that I was always checking to see when they were going to turn the water on. This was not cruelty on their part; the pipes could freeze, and break. My log says that they turned the water back on near the end of March. PTL!

About once a month, after I had my things moved over there, I would meet my friends' wife, and go over to their place for the night. We would have dinner there, and play board games, and talk. We are still friends. I also used to help them with some of their projects.

I remember once when I was there, that the man's wife said to me, "I've got a noise in my car." She was right, the main wire from the center tower on the distributor cap, to the center of the coil, had broken. The spark was jumping an inch or more, which was the sound she had heard. I told her, "You are walking and don't know it." I'm surprised that it ran at all. This was the same kind of problem that I had had with the old Pinto. We found some wire, and made a temporary fix, but the coil had to be replaced.

In early April my friends located another project for me. It seems that a missionary lady had advertised for someone to help fix some donated sewing machines, and other Items. This kept me busy going back and forth from near Philomath, to Albany. The lady gave me bus fare, so I could go back and forth.

In mid April, when I was involved with the missionary ladies work, my father let me know that he had cancer, and would have to have an operation. About a week later I went to my father's place, and spent the night. We got up early, and drove to Salem, Oregon, where the operation was to take place.

My stepmother and I waited a long time, until the Doctor had finished the operation. They had a telephone that he used to talk to us, and told us my father was doing fine. That was a relief! My father was about eighty years old at that time, and I was concerned that the stress of the operation alone could kill him.

My stepmother and I went to the recovery room to wait until he had recovered his faculties. When he woke up I asked him, "How do you feel?" "I feel with my fingers." He told me. (Now you know where I get all these dumb jokes.) He made a full recovery, and has had no recurrence of the cancer. PTL!

I would have my father's car for the next few days, as I had to get him out of the hospital in Salem, and drive him home. (My stepmother didn't drive.) I used the car to move things around, and drive to Albany, to work on the missionary ladies stuff. When I wasn't using the car, I left it with a friend, near where I used to live.

Late in April I finished the work for the missionary lady. I had not done much for the sewing machines, but had fixed some typewriters, bicycles, and some other things. Just about everything was mechanical, as there was little or no electricity in the area she was going to.

She had a Land Rover four wheel drive vehicle, a lot of clothes, a washer dryer combination, all the things I had been working on, and much besides. All this she packed into a twenty-foot shipping container, and then had it welded shut. This was the only way to keep things from disappearing en route. I got newsletters from her for years, and so heard all about it. She gave me some clothes, including a windbreaker that I still use, and am very thankful for.

On May first I loaded up my bicycle, and went to Salem to pick up my father. When I got to him to his place, I ran my stepmother to the store, and then it was time to bike back to camp.

It was a distance of about twenty-six miles, from my father's place, outside Lebanon, to my camp. I made it in about three hours and fifteen minutes, including a stop in Corvallis to tell my friends how my father was doing.

With the work on the missionary lady's bikes, and a friend of mine's junk collection, I got my start fixing bikes. I did this like I did when I was staying with my father, and fixing lawn mowers, before I was homeless. I would buy or be given bicycles, and make what I could of them. I only sold four in 1992, but the next year was much better.

I was always concerned that I would be told to leave suddenly, and not given time to move my things. To cushion a blow like this, I resolved to hide things in unlikely places. I would stash food supplies, and books like this. Some of the books got wet, and the rats built a nest around the canned goods, but otherwise my fears were in vain.

My mousetrap broke. I looked to see what was wrong, and one of the staples that held the mechanism in place had pulled out. I tried putting it back in, but it just came out again.

I hunted around and found a piece of plywood, about the right size, and put all the pieces of the mousetrap on the new platform. This worked well, until I lost it when I failed to tie it up. I caught fifteen mice there, and quite a few more in the next location, until it walked off. (Now you know why the string I wrote about in chapter one.)

There was a free place to get things in Corvallis, called Vina Moses. You could go there once a month and take two bags of clothes, or whatever. I got more books than clothes there, although I got a sleeping bag, and a foam pad there. I found out later that there was another one called the Family Support Outlet in Philomath. These places were a big help in my struggle to survive.

The ARC thrift store also made a contribution to my survival, as well. It was not how you think; I had to pay for everything, except those items left at the back door. If I had worked enough hours I got a small discount.

A lot of things got left at the back door. These went

to another thrift store, not ARC, to be sold. Of the back door stuff, I got a Basic Institute in Youth Conflicts syllabus, and one other book that was a big help to me in my studies. I had been to Basic Youth years before, but had to give up a lot of things when I moved into the sailboat. Now I had, and still have, another one. It had all the supplemental materials and everything. PTL!

If you saw something come into the thrift store, and as I worked in the back room, I sometimes did, and you wanted it, you could ask one of the other staff members to price it out for you. I got a blanket, and some bikes, and bike parts this way.

One day the shoe lady came back to my work area, and dragged a nearly new pair of Avias under my nose. Someone had waded in the mud with them, and she didn't want to have to clean them. (A long job, with questionable results.) So she sold them to me for a very nominal sum. They fit me perfectly, and I used them for a long time until I finally wore them out. By that time I was getting welfare, and could afford to buy new, good quality shoes. This was an absolute necessity if you needed to walk as much as I did.

One of the things that get neglected when people are taking care of homeless people's needs is shoes. Most of the ones that you get in thrift stores, or discount houses are not worth taking home. (They are OK if you don't do much walking.)

One other thing I got at ARC, and almost didn't, was a pack board. The assistant manager showed it to me, and told me it was three dollars. I said I'd think it over. The next week when I came back it was still there, so I bought it. I used it for years, and it never let me down. (So it's ugly, It works!)

In mid May I got the sleeping bag that I mentioned earlier, at Vina Moses. The fabric was all right, but the seams had blown out, so I had to fix it. It was a summer bag, of all nylon construction.

I had made an all nylon bag in 1979; out of two bags that the liners had wore out in. It had a double zipper, but only used one bag's insulation. I used both bags for the duration of my homeless period. This summer bag was the next step in my continuing effort to be a boat missionary.

Another step in the process of becoming a boat missionary, was the gift of a fancy racing bike. It had been left at some people's house, and had been badly neglected. I took at apart, and did my usual service to it, mostly grease, and get the control cables working. I also installed side racks, and a front basket. It would come in handy on a trip I had planned.

Some of the work I did at ARC thrift was of the maintenance order. It was early in June when I was commissioned to build a display island, and put in a call bell. The bell had to sound in the back room so the manager could come to the front, if needed. They often needed volunteers, with the result that the person on the cash register was all alone up front. They couldn't leave their post to get the manager. The bell solved that problem. It was quite a chore putting the bell in, as I had to string wires, and drill holes, but I got it done.

At one point they added more showroom space, in an empty area next door. In the process I had to build bookshelves in the book room. Instead of my usual four or five hours a day, one day a week, I had to work several days to complete this project. They had a work jamboree, in which a lot of temporary volunteers came and worked.

I went to Corvallis to do some shopping. While I was walking around, I saw a screwdriver in the middle of an intersection. So, risking life and limb, I ran out and grabbed it. It was of the four-bit kind, and it is sitting on my desk as I write this. I used to include this screwdriver in my bicycle tool kit, because of all the different choices. I'm sorry for whoever lost it, but once again, I had no means of returning it. I found a socket extension the same day.

On the sixteenth of June, I loaded up my bike, and hopped on. I rode to Sunflower House and took a shower. I was en route to Eugene from a point about a mile or two east of Philomath. I stopped for lunch at a wayside, about half way between, and went on. You've heard of tender feet, well I was tender all right, but not my feet. My rear end was not used to this, and complained loudly. I got south of Junction City all right, but I would be into the third day of my trip getting back.

The reason I went down there was to see what I could find in the line of a sailboat. I had made up some adds on three by five cards, to put up in suitable locations.

I knew the Lord could provide, all I needed to do was get the Lord, myself, and the right boat together, and the money would show up. I was right too; the only problem was the myself part. I had been studying for quite a while, and by this time I knew I had a problem, but I didn't know what it was.

I was just being stubborn, like, I was so used to looking one way that it would be a while before the Lord could change my viewpoint. It felt like, when He was making these changes, as if He was physically twisting my head, to point in a new direction. It would take years, a lot more twisting, and a lot more study, before I changed direction.

I had peddled to a spot south of Junction City, and pitched my tent for the night. As I did this in the open field, I had to pitch the tent when it was nearly dark to avoid being seen. I had to get up very early for the same reason.

The next morning I went on to Eugene. I was looking for boat brokerages, but found only one. I put some ads out in likely places, and then went on to Fern Ridge Lake. At the lake I put out some more adds, then rested for three hours. By this time my rear end is really giving me some trouble. I had found some bubble packing along the road, which helped, but I was still very sore.

From Fern Ridge Lake I peddled north through Cheshire, and a mile or so beyond. There I pitched my tent for the night. I had to push the bike over the hill, which had given my rear end a break. I camped on an old dike, or railroad bed. Once again I had trouble getting the pegs in. They had made the dike out of rocks, but at least it was out of sight.

The next day I rode back to camp. I started about

49

6:10 AM, and got there about 2:30 PM. I had covered about thirty miles that day, with a two-hour rest. I got no results from the adds I had placed.

The bicycle business started off with a bang. The ARC thrift manager had started a new program of consignments. I had been fixing, and completing bikes for a while, and had some of them on consignment. They would only let me have two at a time there, because of space. When I got back from Eugene, I found that they had sold an expensive bike for me. PTL!

Some of the places that I got bikes from were apartment complexes. Corvallis is a University town, and people come and go a lot. Sometimes when they go they leave a bike behind. At one location they gave me ten bikes. Not all could be repaired, of course, but they were glad to be rid of them. Some of them had been cluttering up their bike racks for years. They checked first to see if the owners were still around. (Who wants a legal hassle?) Other places I got them from were friends, yard sales, junk piles, and second hand stores. Some times I would see a bike or two in someone's yard, and ask if they wanted it, or them removed.

I think this bike work was good for me. I always liked to be busy doing something. The money came in handy too, as I could buy things that I otherwise could not. I kept busy at this all the time I could, until a few weeks before I left the area. This bike work, and the books I was studying, were the things, besides the usual survival activities, that I did with my time during this period. This would change with the fall.

Sunflower House would help you get dental care, so I asked if I could get some help. They made an appointment to get checked out, and another to get fixed. The first appointment was in Corvallis, the second in Albany. During the second appointment they cleaned my teeth, and although I brushed regularly, it had been a long time since the work had been done. The dental hygienist really had her work cut out for her. They also filled one of my teeth.

My father's car had quit over on the coast, so I rode my bike over to his place, and then we went to the coast. The car just needed a tune up, and so I did that. Then he had me drive his pickup back from the coast, and he drove his car. The people at the wrecking yard, who had installed the engine, had not hooked up the warning light. The cooling system developed a leak, and by the time I got to Lebanon with it, the engine had burned up. We still had a short ways to go, but we towed it home all right. When I took it apart I found out that it probably wouldn't have lasted too long anyway.

While I was at my father's, we talked about my early life. It seems that my mother had only nursed me for a brief time. My studies were progressing in the direction of childcare, and how it could affect your later life. Therefore I resolved to buy a book that would give me some idea as to the effect of this situation on myself. I found a book that gave me some input on this, it was on breast-feeding, and gave me some ideas.

As I knew I had a problem, I thought that if I solved my problem, the Lord would move on the boat ministry. So I went down to the County Mental Health Clinic, and made an appointment.

When I shared the information about my mother only nursing me for a brief time, I was told that there would be problems bonding to my mother. It makes sense; I've always had this feeling of being a stranger to my mom. It goes like this, I know (think) she's my mom, but I feel (emotion) like she's a stranger. It's kind of difficult to sort out.

In early September I could see that I was going to spend yet another winter in the woods, so I worked very hard to stock up the place. I bought canned pork and beans, cereal, and peanut butter, among other items.

My regular counseling sessions started in late September. They were interrupted by frequent cancellations. Single men had a low priority, and if a family was in trouble, I got cancelled. The problem was that they couldn't call me, so I would arrive, only to be told my session had been canceled. They were canceled out completely around Christmas time. After Christmas we got down to business.

There were, in my experience, two different kinds of

these County Mental Health Clinics. The one in Corvallis was too busy; their focus seemed to be to get the person out the door as quickly as possible. The result was positive, but superficial.

The second kind, in North Bend, Oregon, wasn't busy enough. There the emphasis seemed to be to keep the person in the system as long as possible. The people that worked there felt that to maintain a caseload was to justify their continued employment, or so it seemed.

Of the two I would prefer the first. I did not know all this then. If not for my continued studies, I would not have made any progress in my search for truth, after I went to the Coos Bay area. I've put this in here so that my readers who want to make progress in their own life search, can make a swift assessment of the situation, and so not waste any more time than necessary.

The people at the Corvallis clinic would at least tell me things. They made suggestions as to books I could study, including a suggestion to study a book on assertiveness. They gave me a referral to the anger management course, at the Sunflower House. I identified my problem as anger. Why I was angry was a total mystery. Managing anger doesn't help much if you don't know why you are angry. More on this later.

In early October the hunters once again visited me. This time they didn't want me gone, they were just suspicious of all those bikes. They had called the Police, and the Officer had come out, and was about to investigate, when I came back from some errand. He looked the situation over, checked out one bike, then left. I was very thankful that I didn't have to move again. This was especially so as I had a lot of bikes ready for next year.

In mid October I got the flu, and didn't feel well for about a week. I was drinking out of water jugs, and because I had been sick, I would now have to rinse them all out. I've had problems like this before, and if you don't rinse out your water jugs, you take a chance on re-infecting yourself.

Sometime in early October I bought a one-burner

camp stove. It was on sale, or I couldn't have afforded it. I wanted to heat water for those Chinese noodle soups, and also hot chocolate. (I don't drink coffee.) It turned out to be a lifesaver when the snow was on. If I hadn't bought it I think I would have frozen. I've still got it and I use it when I'm on a trip, or just want to get away.

Some time in early October I discovered a free place to get things called the Family Support Outlet. They were a Christian based help service. I don't remember getting much from them in the way of clothes, but I did get some books there. I also organized their book department. They were only open certain days of the week, and you could only go there once a month. They were nice people who really wanted to help.

There was a lot of snow and cold weather in the winter of 1992-93. Despite the snow and the cold, I managed to get water and food in. My logbook says that I made two trips to a friend's place for water, about sixteen miles total. I packed four gallons of water each time. I'm too old now, and could never do it again. It had been too wet and snowy to get out and get the things I needed. The old saying about making hay while the sun shines certainly applied.

In mid January of 1993, I applied for the anger management course at the Sunflower House. It would take a lot of maneuvering to get to get this course. They weren't able to tell me why I was angry, but I still got a lot of useful stuff out of it.

The Sunflower House had a message board, and when I went to check it, I found that my father had had a stroke. The next day I got on the bus from Corvallis to Albany, and then walk the rest of the way to my father's place, near Lebanon. I can be thankful, even though it's February, the weather is good.

When I walked up, my father was about to climb up a ladder to fix the roof. I immediately assumed this chore, as I didn't think too much of someone climbing up on a roof right after a stroke!!!

He couldn't talk to well, or walk to well, but he was

making do. As time went along he got better, but never recovered fully. The next day I reversed the trip, arriving just before it started raining. PTL! Another of the many times I got back to my shelter before it rained.

The resident psychiatrist at the Mental Health Clinic wanted to try to calm me down. To this end he prescribed lithium. The only problem with it was that it gave me bells in my head. I called about this, and finally found out that I could quit the pills. It would be years before the bells left though. I don't know whether anyone else has this problem, with this medication, or not.

When I went to the park in Philomath in mid March, I didn't find any water. What I did find was two space cases, (milk crates) in the Dumpster, at the park. I used them for years, and finally sold one of them in a yard sale. I used the other one to hold up my TV for a long time, but now I have found a different use for it. They are very recycle conscious in Oregon. I found some soap buckets, at about this time, that I'm still using. Someone had put them out to be picked up for recycle. Well, I'm sure that what I did with them wasn't quite what they would have expected, but I did recycle them.

One of the things that I had to do all through my homeless period, was turn in a monthly change report. This report was due at the Adult and Family services office on a certain day of the month, or you wouldn't get any food stamps. If it was late, so would be your food stamps. I know that some homeless people move around a lot, so they didn't know whether you would be there the next month or not.

This particular organization was different than the usual bureaucracy, in that they would tell you things so that you could make the system work better in your interest. Whether this is still so I don't know. The way things usually go, it may not be so. When dealing with any strange bureaucracy, the safest course is to ask a lot of questions of a general nature.

In mid May, I started the anger management course. It was in the evening, and took about three hours an evening, with a break in the middle. They held it once a week. To start with the two instructors gave their resumes. In the process of the resume sharing I discovered that one of them had been to the same islands that I had been on.

At break I told her that, I too, had been on this island. When we compared notes, one of the things she said was, "There are no crying children on those islands." This fit into my observations as well.

She also said, "The people there don't compete with each other." "Family group will compete with family group, but they don't compete on an individual to individual basis."

Through my studies I have found why this is so. IF each child gets enough positive, focused, emotional attention, they won't be mean to each other. If each child gets this kind of attention, it will eliminate sibling, and other rivalries. So much for competition.

The problem starts in infancy, the child needs attention, and if it is not immediately available, the child will cry, squall, or throw things to get attention. If the child can't meet it's needs this way it becomes passive. This behavior is carried over into later childhood, and adulthood. Of course the new child will resent any sharing of attention with any other child, and vice versa, if any child is not getting enough attention.

There is a story I read. (I can't remember the source.) It seems a long time ago in Eastern Europe; there lived a king. This King, (Fredric the Great of Prussia?) wanted to find out what the original human language was. He then commissioned some people to take newborn foundlings, and feed and care for them. They were not to talk to them, or around them. The result? They all, without exception, died. This is the final stage of the neglect syndrome.

I know myself to be a relatively passive person. I know also that my parents were the result of two dysfunctional families. From this I can deduce that they did not have the care, from their parents, to care for me. More on this later.

The island women carry their children everywhere, and don't use diapers. So if the child wets or defecates, the mother knows all about it long before the child needs to cry to make its needs known. The same goes for feeding, the child nuzzles the mom, the mom rearranges her garments, and nursing takes place.

The big plus is that someone is always there for the child. If the mom is unavailable, either one of the relatives take over, or one of the older brothers or sisters. Neighbors and friends are also part of the extended family.

The point is that the child doesn't have to be mean to others to meet its attention needs. Because of this early, close interaction with others, this person, when grown, will, in turn, have emotional attention to give.

If you wish to see this in action, you can get a movie called; "The Gods Must be Crazy." There is a second movie, with this title, as well. Although the pattern of play is different, and the people's lifestyles are too, the attitude is the same. (Both movies are very funny, as well.)

During the period when I was going to anger management, I sometimes got to the Sunflower House a little early. The house had a picnic table in the back, and I would wait there for the classes to start. One day while waiting, one of the homeless people was talking about being hassled by the Police. He was trying to sleep in his car, and was told to leave. I made a comment, out of the blue, and I said, "It seems a rent receipt in this country is a license to live."

Someone had donated a small transistor radio at ARC, and I asked one of the other staff members to price it for me. I bought it, as my old radio had quit. The Bible says to watch, but it's difficult when you don't know what is going on in the world. I could get weather reports as well.

Another thing that got donated, were some sox. They were all the same, except one pair. My log says that I bought them for seventy-five cents. One of the staff members found them in a donation, and called my attention to them. This was late in June of '93. As I write this I'm wearing the last of them, in December of '00. PTL!

Two other things I got out of the classes on anger management. You can't go back and meet the needs you had as a child, although many try. The other is a list of feelings you can have besides anger. (I may have gotten more than this, but I can't remember any more. I still have my notes, maybe I should look at them!) The program lasted two months, one night a week.

I had completed anger management, and although I still had problems, I wanted to see if it was time for the Lord to work. So once again I biked my way down to Eugene to see about finding a boat. This time I installed a wider seat, and tied some foam to it, so it wasn't nearly so much of a hassle. I made it to Eugene by early afternoon, and put out two ads. Then I peddled back north, and camped near Clear Lake road. I had traveled about forty-five miles that day.

I spent most of the next day at the parks near Fern Ridge Lake, and then I started north. I was met by rain showers, and spent some time under the over hang of an old service station/store. It wasn't being used for either one of those purposes but it was someone's house. Nobody complained, and when the rain let up I was on my way. I got to my old campsite, that I had used the year before, about dark.

I spent a very soggy night, and went on my way the next day. I arrived tired, but a lot more quickly than last year. It took me about four hours, and forty-five minutes to get back to my camp. Once again I got no results from my ads. The Lord was trying to tell me something, but I haven't got the message yet.

In early August I walked to the ledge campsite, west of Blodgett. I found a cold chisel on the way. The chisel would come in handy when I built a stove in one of my future camps. I needed to think things over, and walking helps the process.

I returned the next day, having come to some conclusions. The hunters would be back in the area I was camping in next fall, and who knows what the result of that might be. I had been working with the same group of people for some time, and this had not worked well in the past. (I was starting to make sharp comments, a sign that I was emotionally stressed.) I had been in the same area too long,

57

never a good idea when you are homeless.

So where do I go from here? I had already been looking around the area to find another campsite, but no go. In fact I had been looking since I had got there. It's not easy finding suitable campsites.

If I was going to leave the area I had much to do. The bike parts had to be disposed of, I had to build a wheelbarrow out of bike parts, I had to select a new area to go to, and I had to scout it. I also must pass my work on to someone at the thrift store.

My father has a van, and I can borrow it for a short time to move with. The bikes have sold well, so I have some money to pay for gas and bus tickets. I can also buy building materials for my new shelter.

The last day I work at ARC thrift store, they have some new volunteers. They are two seventh grade girls, which I kid around a lot. They were very sad when I said I wouldn't be working there anymore.

These parent's who don't show much attention to their kids, leave their kids vulnerable to someone who shows them some attention. This especially is true of girls who don't get any attention from their fathers. They are likely to take up with the first man who shows them some attention.

One of the ladies at the thrift store was talking about her daughter. She said that her daughter didn't show much interest in men until she got to college. I asked her, "How much attention did she get from her father?" "A lot," was the reply. (You can give a child too much attention, or attention of the wrong kind.)

How I moved, and what happened when I did, and how I survived, is the subject of the next chapter.

Chapter Six

I have made a choice of a new area to move to, now to inspect it to see if my ideas will work in the real world. So I load my pack board with all the things I will need for a stay of some days in the woods. Then I buy a bus ticket, and away I go. It is late August of 1993, and I am fifty years old.

The first bus takes me to Newport, Oregon, and then I have to wait, until the second one takes me south. On the second bus there is this lady, and her daughter, who are sitting in front of me. The mom is talking to the bus driver, and the daughter, who is about two years old, focuses her attention on me. The little girl is talking, but mostly in baby talk. The little girl hands me her doll, which I give to the mom, who gives it to the child again.

I've got about a hundred miles to go to Coos Bay, Oregon, which is my destination. This play goes on for quite a while between the child and myself. I have asked the bus driver if he will let me off a little ways before the scheduled stop, and so he does, but when I get off that bus the child throws a fit.

Through my studies I have learned that the opposite sex parent is the most important in the development of the child. Both parents are necessary, but for girls the father is the most important. This reverses itself after the child, of either sex, is about five years of age.

What had happened was I, a man, had paid attention to the girl, and for a little while, met a genuine need. When the attention giver was taken away, the child felt deserted. Someone liked the little girl, and now he was gone. I realized what I had done and felt very badly about it. I prayed to God that He would find someone to meet this child's needs, and be there to care for her.

The pack I'm carrying weighs about fifty pounds, and as I'm fifty years old, this requires a rest every couple of miles or so. I went down the beach on the inside of the bay, but no go; there was a paper mill there. Then I went back to the road, and tried again. The map I had was out of date by quite a bit; they had built a whole road, pavement and all. I walked down this for a ways, and I believe, guided by the Lord, found a place to set up my next camp.

To get to the campsite you have to climb up a one hundred-foot high sand hill that had been baloney sliced out of a hill when they built the road. Some effort had been made to sow grass on the sand, but it was still partly sand. The top of the hill, and the area in a kind of gully that reached to the road, was grown up to all kinds of vegetation. There were fir trees, white cedar trees, rhododendron, huckleberry, and pine trees. When you got close to the top, you could crowd your way past some small rhododendrons, walk along a log, and find yourself on a trail of sorts. A walk through the woods of about a hundred yards would bring you to my camp area. I was very pretty, mostly green and brown, with big trees, and little pine squirrels to squeak at you.

I immediately set up a temporary camp, as it was getting close to the end of the day. I had purchased a new, and very large green tarp, (I always used green tarps. They helped camouflage my camp, and the skylight effect minimized eyestrain.) Which I used for this temporary camp, as well as the more permanent one.

I had determined on a new design for my shelter. The old "A" frame had worked, but not too well. You couldn't stand up in there with the bunk in, and it didn't have room for all my stuff.

The new design went like this, eight foot by eight foot floor, walls about forty inches high, and the peak of the roof about nine feet tall. This pattern worked well, and I used this design for later shelters as well.

The day after I arrived I got busy, and found some dead trees that were standing up. The timber was very tall, so young trees tended to grow up tall and skinny, and tended to die quickly. I found several that were about the right length, and about four inches or less in diameter.

These poles would be stringers in my new shelter. Stringers run horizontally along a set of rafters, and mount whatever roofing is being used. I used these to give the tarp some support.

That day I also took a four and a half-hour walk around the area, and found a water supply. In the following days I would search the beaches and the area for lumber. I found enough to panel the back end wall with plywood, and frame up the sidewalls.

When I was walking in from the highway, I saw two sheets of foam insulation floating in the bay. I went back for them, but the wind blows very hard on sunny days, and the insulation was very light, so they blew right out of my hands. I couldn't get them back that afternoon. I went back one morning, when the winds were calmer, and packed them back.

I took a day off from my project and walked to Coos Bay. I wanted to check on the location of, stores, social service agencies, thrift shops, post offices, and anything else that might help me survive. I was also interested in getting some more counseling, as what I had been through didn't get the job done. I don't remember whether I checked on this then though.

On one of the days when I went out on the beach looking for lumber, I found a one by four-inch board, four-teen feet long. I didn't have enough poles for stringers, and this would finish up the job. I packed the board back by road, and as I was walking along, some old men stopped in a pickup. They asked me, "What are you doing?" "I've been a victim of piracy," I replied, "I'm walking the plank." They laughed and went on.

The day I left, I went to get some short boards early, and packed them back. Then I took a spit bath, and walked to the bus station. Before I left I tied my pack board to a tree, in such a way that it would be difficult to see. By the time I got back to Philomath I had been gone six days.

I did not want to move during Labor Day weekend, and I wanted to wait to move until after school had begun. I needed more lumber than I had, and I wanted to get the best price, so I walked around a lot to locate the things I needed. Although I had some money left from the bike sales, I couldn't just throw money around. Most of the time between when I got back and when I moved was occupied with shopping, or carting things to a point near the road where I could stash them, in my home made wheelbarrow.

On the seventh of September, I took my bike to my father's place. I helped with a project of theirs', and checked out the van for the trip. I had to buy a radiator hose for the van before I could go, but otherwise the van was ready.

I made several stops in Albany and Corvallis, to pick up lumber and food supplies. I went to the next stage of the move when I picked up the things I had left near my old camp. Then I drove to the area that I planned to camp in, North of the Coos Bay/ North Bend cities.

I picked up some boards that I had left near the road, and then start unloading the van. This was quite a process, and I would stash most of it in the brush and small trees at the bottom of the hill. I had hoped to carry it all up the hill before I went back to Lebanon, but that proved to be beyond my strength. The items I unloaded, and partly packed up the hill were these, sixteen or more 2"x4"x8' boards, four sheets of 1/2" plywood, several dozen cans of pork and beans, a lot of granola cereal, a lot of books, plus some tools, a bike, some clothes and a lot of etc.

The reason I described the hill, and the trail through the woods, was to give you some idea of what I was facing. Packing all this up the hill in the dark was not going to happen in one night! I was eating licorice for energy, and ducking out of sight every time I saw car lights. I got so tired that I thought I was going to barf, but I didn't. By 2:30 AM I had gotten some of the things moved up the hill, and some of the lumber. It would be enough to continue the work when I got back.

I drove from where I had been unloading back to the valley. I had to turn off the P.O. Box, at Philomath, and take the van back to my father. My father took me back to Philomath, and I slept for the last time in the old "A" frame.

The following day was Friday the tenth of September. I got the bus back to near my location, arriving fairly early in the day. I walked from where I was dropped off to my new campsite, and found that nothing had been touched.

The remainder of the day was spent cutting the foundation logs. These were old cedar trees that had fallen. The bark was gone, but the wood was sound. I used one ten-foot piece, and two shorter ones. (The tree had broken when it fell.) My logbook says that I got one frame of the floor in that day.

About midnight I got up and walked to where I had the lumber stashed at the bottom of the hill. I made seven loads that night, mostly of lumber. Although there was a kind of misty drizzle, it never rained until long after I had gotten my work done. I didn't know that things would work out that way, so I was in a hurry to get my shelter built before it started raining.

Except for trips for stashes of lumber near the bayside beach, and for water, this would be my routine until I got my shelter done: Up in the middle of the night to get lumber, or supplies. Work all the daylight hours to build the shelter.

I remember that I had located some plywood that had been dumped. It had been part of a home-built camper, or storage shed. I cleaned off the tar and roofing, and I used it on the back end wall. There were two pieces of this 5/8" plywood, one was not too big, but the other was nearly a full sheet. It was very heavy, and nearly killed me getting it up the hill. I had to stop and rest a lot, but I did it. PTL!

By September fifteenth I was moved in, and although I would put the finishing touches on for a while, it could rain if it wanted to.

I had to get my food stamps coming to the new area I was in, and some other things done. One problem that I had was that I couldn't get a P.O. box in North Bend. It seems that they had no boxes available, and even if they did, they would only rent to North Bend residents, and no others. As I didn't have a rent receipt, I was out. I would get my mail general delivery for the next year or so.

Now that I was installed in my new location, I decided to take a walk around. I walked the inside of the bay to the FFA place, and to get back, I walked in the dunes. In the process I found some rope, and a length of stovepipe, with an elbow. The stovepipe would come in handy some time later.

On the twenty-first of September, I took my bike and rode to Charleston, Oregon. It is located near the mouth of Coos Bay. I went to see if I could find a sailboat to do missionary work with. I did some shopping in route. After I got back I went for water, and brought back four gallons and a quart. My logbook says that I was very tired, which happened a lot about this time, what with the moving and all.

One day in early October, I found a flashlight as I was returning from town. It even worked! I'm still using it, and it's been a big help. It finally broke in 2003.

I was walking around the area, and found a new place to get water. The park people have a horse camp, for those who want to ride horseback around the area. It was rarely used, and had several spigots, so that's where I went for water. There was a trail that started a quarter of a mile from where I got down off the hill that led right to it. The trail was very handy, as nobody could see me going to get water. Later in the year they turned off the water to prevent the pipes from breaking if it froze.

I had heard on the radio that they were going to have a beach cleanup. This occurred on Friday, October the eighth. On the way over there, I stashed some water jugs, so that I could fill them on the way back. A bunch of people showed up for the work. We wandered up and down the beach picking up, and cataloging the trash we found. I had brought a lunch, and then discovered that they had hot dogs, and juice. Oh Well!

It seems the hunters are different in this area, instead of deer, they pick mushrooms. (Imagine, picking on those poor little mushrooms!) The way I found out about this was that some of the mushroom pickers visited me. Every thing was cool; the man was a really nice dude. He told me where he lived, and over the time I was in the area, we became acquainted. I even visited him, but only after I had gotten off the street.

Late in October I went for a walk. I went down the inside of the bay to the jetty, then back up the ocean side. In the process I found what I thought might be human remains. There had been a boat lost sometime before, and I thought that this might be some of the body parts. There wasn't much, just part of a rib cage.

I looked the spot over carefully, so I could find it again. Then I went to the BLM boat launch ramp, and called the County Sheriffs office. It was a while before anyone could respond, as there had been a plane crash that day. Eventually someone showed up, but no four-wheel drive. A BLM ranger was in the area, and he ran us out on the beach to look at the bones. They took them away to be tested, but I never did find out whether they were human or not.

I was always walking around, so early in November I walked north, up highway 101. I found a lot of things, among them a glove. It was a very warm glove, but there was only one of them. I picked it up hoping that I could find the other one, but no go. The next day I walked into town to go to the grocery store, and there was the other glove! I've used them a lot, and still have them. I hope the person that lost them could replace them easily, and without breaking the bank. Once again I had no means of finding the owner.

About this time I saw something that will probably never forget. Here was a mom and two children in the grocery store. The older child was about tall enough that her head was level with the grocery cart handle, of the cart she was pushing. The mom was talking to the younger child, a boy. The mom was saying, "I'm going to hold you, but I have to do this shopping."

The boy was about two, and at that age, a child has no time sense. So to say later to a child at that age, is to say NO. One incident like this will not greatly damage the child. But if the mom is forced to make a choice between meeting the children's emotional needs, and other family duties, it could prove devastating to the children's emotional development. Such is our civilization. The pacific islanders would not have had a problem. Someone would have held the child, while the mom did the shopping.

Early in November I found a gray pullover fleece. It was very greasy, so I dropped it off at the dry cleaners. It cost four dollars to clean it, but I've been using it ever since, including today as I type this. I don't think it was lost, someone just tossed it rather than clean it. I've made good use of their trash. Other than the grease, it was, and is in good condition. All the grease came out, and it was clean.

I still wasn't getting anywhere with the boat ministry, so I decided to get some more counseling. I still thought that if I could get my problems sorted out I could get on with the work. To this end I went to the Coos County Mental Health Clinic in North Bend, Oregon. I started this process on November eighteenth, of '93.

This operation was different, they wanted money! Something I had little of, and none to spare. They told me two things, that they wouldn't refuse me service, and that if I was found to be disabled by the State of Oregon, I could pay their fees.

A few days later I went to the Senior and Disabled Services office, and applied for benefits. They said that I was going to have to be tested by a clinical psychologist, and we made a series of two appointments. They told me they would have someone pick me up, and take me to the appointments. The other thing that they required was that I had to apply for disability through the Social Security Administration. They said that they could recover the costs, and welfare paid to me, from them.

I was very interested in the results of the tests, as the more that I knew about myself; the better I might work with any therapy I might get. I could also figure out what to do with myself, as far as the Lord's work was concerned.

During the winter months I got water at two locations, the boat launch ramp, and the off road camp ground. I alternated between the two, as I didn't want to be hassled.

They were about two miles from my camp, by road, but in opposite directions. They started digging ponds for the waterfowl about this time, which wrecked the trail to the horse camp, so I never went there for water again.

All the time I was homeless I regularly got my hair cut. It wasn't often, about every three or four months. This was part of my invisibility program. If you look like a bum, you'll probably be treated like one. If you look like you have some respect for yourself, others may respect you too.

On the fourteenth of December I went to town. It wasn't raining when I started, and it wasn't raining when I got back, but it poured in the middle. I started early, about 6:30 AM, and walked the four miles or so to the County Mental Health clinic. I had an eight-o-clock appointment with a therapist. (I'll call him "P".) That took about half an hour.

I had an afternoon appointment with the Social Security people. Between appointments I shopped for used books, and groceries.

It was still pouring rain, and I didn't use any rain gear. I had it, but didn't use it much. I had found that if you walked while wearing it, you wound up just as wet, and smelling worse, than if you hadn't worn the rain gear at all. The sweat from the exercise of walking is what got you wet. I smelled much better with just being wet with rainwater. (I took a spit bath, and used deodorant, before I went to town.) I always used an umbrella, as this would keep the upper part of me dry.

On the day I'm talking about nothing was going to stay dry, as the wind was blowing very hard. It was one of those days that it rains up at you, as the saying goes. By the time I got to the Mental Health Clinic, I was soaked, and would remain so the rest of the day. The only way to survive a situation like this is to keep exercising, or to stay in a warm, dry place. I always walked at a three mile per hour pace, and it paid off on this day. I wasn't warm, but I did survive.

My appointment with the Social Security people was in the mid afternoon. There was a hang up with someone with a previous appointment, so by the time I got out of there it was nearly dark, and about a half hour past closing time. I went back by the long route, as I still had some shopping to do. I finally got back to my camp after seven PM.

It had been a very long day, and I was exhausted. You can use a lot of energy fighting the cold and wind. I stripped off my soaked clothes, toweled down, and went to bed. I woke up at about two AM. What had awakened me? My feet were warm, and the change in the temperature of my feet had awakened me. This happened all the time during the cold months.

The next day was the first of two appointments with the clinical psychologist. I am one of those people who hate to be late, so I had scheduled the pick up time a lot earlier than necessary. It was a good thing, as the people who were supposed to pick me up didn't show. I called my caseworker, A Mr. Hardt, and he came and picked me up. A local business helped me in that they borrowed me their telephone. The nearest pay phone was miles away.

On the way over to the appointment I asked Mr. Hardt, "Have you heard the new definition of a person on a fixed income?" "No," he replied, "The only one I know about is the one where the person only has so much money coming in a month." "The new definition is this," I told him, "A person's income was broke, so they fixed it." (It was "fixed.")

The tests took about four hours that day, and seemed to be testing my intelligence, as well as other things. There was no rain that day, for which I was thankful. I walked back.

I was going to town about every day at this time, as I was trying to keep all these balls in the air. This was not good for my invisibility, as I was being seen too much. I was concerned lest someone notice, and ask questions. No one did though.

The day after my first session with the clinical psychologist, I went to my first session of group therapy. For those of my readers who have never been to one of these sessions I will share some of what went on, but none of the personalities that were there.

This is one of the rules; nothing of what is shared goes beyond the door. Another rule is that only first names are used. Mostly people shared their problems, or how they felt, or what was hassling them. The group would talk about it, and sometimes make suggestions as to what to do. Sometimes the moderator would start the conversation by asking a person how they felt about someone or something, and then the group could discuss it. With my growing knowledge of human behavior, I sometimes talked about possible causes for problems. The psychologists who ran the show rarely ever made any suggestions as to what might be wrong, or how to fix it, either in group, or in private therapy sessions.

Sometimes the moderator would do something different. Once they asked the people in the group to share a poem. This poem, which I shared, was written by me in the Mojave Desert in the early '80s.

You can live in the city where loneliness holds sway, and trouble and heartache have their way,

But I'll look to the mountains, or the vastness of the sea, the solitude of the desert, and there in peace I'll be.

O won't you look around you; there are so many things to buy,

But don't you wonder, do I need them, and why?

For most things in life there is neither need nor cause, but toys for age-ed children, to ease the doubt that gnaws.

For there is only God and man and the labor that is done, and loneliness is just foolishness as you walk under the sun.

I set this poem to music, and still have the tune available, but I could never sing it anymore, as my voice is not what it used to be.

The second appointment with the clinical psychologist was upon me, this time the caseworker said he would pick me up. Once again I made my arrangements with time to spare, and once again I was left waiting at the altar. I walked very fast, and made it with three minutes to spare. I wasn't very happy, and I don't know what effect this had on the tests. I got it done, however.

The next day I went to group therapy, and then to see my caseworker. I asked him what had happened, and he said, "I forgot." The main reason I went over there was to find out if I could see the results of the tests. He said no to that.

I was finally able to learn what they thought of me when I got the determination back from Social Security. This was years later. I needed the information to plan my life, and was very unhappy when this was denied me. (I was to find that most psychologists would not tell you anything about yourself, except the positive stuff. This smacks of flattery.)

If I had not been studying my books, I never would have found out what I needed to know. I would have still beating my head against the brick wall of a life that wouldn't work normally. You need to know what your problems are, before you can plan your life around the reality of the person you are.

My new camp has a problem that I had not foreseen, mice. I discovered I had a problem on the evening of Christmas Day. Scritch, scritch, scritch, on the table. I turned on the flashlight, and it left. Then once again in a few minutes, mouse noises.

I got up and found the mousetrap, and set it. In a few minutes, snap! I turned on the flashlight and found that I had caught the perpetrator. I figured out where they were getting in, and fixed it over the next few days.

The area was infested with mice! One evening before eleven PM, I caught five, outside the shelter. In all the times I was there I caught something like seventy-five mice. Only three or four ever got inside, that I know of.

On the twenty-seventh of December, I took a walk

north up highway 101. Among the items I found was a wristwatch. After you cross the viaduct, as you travel west, there is a sandy area where people pulled off to park. As I was walking back to my campsite, I found this watch lying there. There was nothing on the face, just a blank. I hammered it on my arm, and it started working. It has never stopped, and is in my pocket as I write this. (Watch bands last quick with me, so I use it as a pocket watch.) It is a fancy timer watch, and for a long time I used it for an alarm clock. Thank You Lord for the Christmas present, as if Your Son was not enough. (After I had written this I realized that it was seven years to the day, from the time I found the watch, until I wrote about it.)(It finally quit in May of 04.)

These were my hopes for the New Year. (1994)

1) Disability to fund a better habitation. (?)

2) Sore throat to heal.

3) Help sort out my emotions.

4) More work on personal message.

5) Leading of the Lord in future missions, relationships.

6) Project, or projects to keep me busy, and earn money.

I had several ideas as to what the projects might be, but the only one that looks likely is the book. I didn't start this until November of the year two thousand.

On January sixth of '94, I got my first welfare check from Senior and Disabled Services. This shows how fast you could be assessed, now if only the Social Security administration would do something like this. The State of Oregon has a law that says that they have to process your claim in two months. Too bad the Social Security Administration isn't required to do likewise.

The next thing that I had to do, now that I had money, was find a bank to put it in. I wanted one that was multi-state, so that if I moved, I could still function financially. After surveying the choices, I chose one with a low cost account. As long as I used the ATM machine, I didn't have any account fees, and my checks were free. (I had to pay for the personalized checks, but there was no charge if I wrote any.) I used my friend's address in Corvallis, as a homeless person is not supposed to have a checking account.

I could now pay the mental health clinic what I owed them. I had to pay a nominal sum, each time I went, (I can't remember how much.) and I was several payments behind. The first check was enough to pay my entire bill, and have quite a bit left.

There was a log near the entrance to the trail that led to my campsite. It was nicely situated because it was exposed to the sun from the south. The hill was overgrown with trees and shrubs, and sheltered the area of the log from the wind. When you get sunshine on the coast, you can get this cold north wind. I would go out to the log and sit in the sun until it went behind some trees. I wasn't too comfortable, but it beat sitting in that cold, damp shelter. (The shelter didn't leak, it's just damp on the coast.)

Late in January, I went for a walk on the beach. Among the other items I found was a plastic box that had held 1/4" drive sockets. There were no sockets in it, and I had to cut the corners out of it to let the sand out, but it was a good little box to organize my sockets in. I still have it.

Every Thursday I went to group therapy, during this period. I also had some counseling sessions with "P." I was finally getting into a routine, and didn't have to go places so much, which helped my invisibility.

As I was walking into town to the group meeting, late in January, I found a sixteen-foot tape measure. It was in good condition, but smelled of diesel fuel. I still have it, and as I eventually got rid of all the others that I had, I'm glad to have found it. Once again, no way to return it.

The route to town was across two viaducts, and two bridges. They were exposed to wind and weather. The concrete pavement on the bridges had sections in it, and when the vehicles went across these sections, they went bump, bump, bump. If anything was left loose on the vehicles, it would be shook off. I found the most amazing things on these bridges. I always kept an eye out when I crossed, and usually found something, even if it was only hardware. More about this later.

I was told to see if I could get low income housing at the County Housing Department. They told me that they only took applications when they did. I asked them when they did, and they said they didn't know. I asked them if they would tell me when they knew, and they said they didn't do that.

I'm sure this process worked well for the people that worked there, but not for someone who was homeless. To be told something like this is very frustrating. It seemed that they were running this department for them, and not for the people they were supposed to be serving.

I later found out that unless you had a priority, single men didn't get housing for about six years. Even with a priority it took about a year and a half. To get a priority you had to be disabled, and not just the State of Oregon either, it had to be from the Social Security Administration. It was like being told NEVER in a nice way.

In early February the new Oregon Health Plan got started. It covered just about everything. Medical, dental, optical, and mental health were all covered. The dental didn't do much good in this area, as there weren't enough dentists to go around. I no longer had to pay the monthly amount at the mental health clinic.

This goes to show the providence of the Lord. If I had started this process a few months later, I wouldn't have had to get welfare to pay for my care. I wouldn't have had to apply for disability at the Social Security either. This means that I could be still on the street, and this book would never be written.

Late in February, "P" my therapist, took me to the County Housing place, but the result was the same as before. I don't know whether these people don't care, or the regulations under which they work won't let them care effectively.

73

The day after I went to see about housing with the therapist, I checked out a hotel in Coos Bay. There was too much interaction to suit me. I probably would not have been able to cope with all the people. I don't think I had such a clear idea of my problems then, I just felt trapped by all the people staying there.

One of the things that "P" suggested, was a place called Peoples Thrift. It was a combination of thrift store, counseling, and day use area for people with problems. I was assigned to a lady I will call "S," as a worker. They tried to come up with a place to stay on my limited income. (At that time $275.00 monthly.)"S" gave me several free rides back to my camp area. She told me that if I had to move to get in touch with her.

On one of these trips back to my camp area, we got to talking about her kids. Seems one of them had had an extended illness, and now was well. The only problem was that now the child couldn't concentrate on homework. The thing was that while the child was sick, there had been a lot of TV viewing by the child.

I shared something that I had read in a newspaper sometime before. It seems that people get used to so many sense impressions per second. Television provides over two thousand, homework, only a few hundred. That's why the child couldn't concentrate, too few sense impressions. Sometime later I rode with "S" again, and I inquired about the child and the homework problem. I was told that they had left the TV on, with the home shopping network as a background. It was something too boring to look at, but it gave a background of added sense impressions. Now the child could concentrate.

The Social Security turned down my first attempt to get into their system in early March. I mailed the appeal the day I got the turn down, and hoped that I would be success-ful.

The same day that I filed the appeal, I rented a stor-age unit from a real estate office. The only one that I could find available was about ten miles from my campsite. It was a five by ten-foot area. I wanted it because I had hopes of getting off the street. I wanted to accumulate some furniture, as well as pick up my belongings that I had in my friend's attic. I wanted to be ready when an opportunity showed up.

Early in the morning of the eighth of March Of 1994, I walked to the bus depot, in North Bend. From there I went to Newport, where I changed buses. On the second bus I went to Lebanon, and walked from Lebanon the two miles to my father's place. (Actually it was more my stepmother's place than it was my father's. My stepmother had owned the property before my father had married her.)

I spent some time fixing, and servicing the van they had. My father and stepmother gave me some furniture that they had stored in the back of their property, in a shed that they had. I can only remember a dinning room table, but there were some other items, as well.

When I had wheels, I really shopped out! The next day I went to Albany, and bought books, groceries, and a recliner chair. I got the recliner in a junk shop for ten bucks. On to Corvallis, to buy more books. Then on to Philomath, to buy more books, a chest of drawers, and end tables.

By this time the van is getting full, and I still have to get my belongings from my friend's place! I went to my friends, and loaded my things, plus a bed that he gave me. We had dinner at his place, then I drove the hundred and fifty miles or so to my camp area, North of the Coos Bay. Somehow I managed to get it all in.

It was late at night when I got to my camp area, which suited me fine. Nobody was around to see what I was doing. I picked up some chairs that somebody had dumped, and unloaded the groceries, which included packing the groceries up the hill. By the time I got this chore done it was early morning, and I'm very tired. I don't know whether I got any sleep that night or not, but if I did it wasn't much.

When daylight came, I went to Coos Bay to check with some agencies that might locate a dwelling for me. These were Community Action, and Peoples Thrift. Then I went to the storage unit, and unloaded. I checked around some more, and then I drove back to my father's place.

When I got back to my father's place, he had a project for me. He had built a prefabricated shed, and wanted to isolate it from the pasture. To do that he needed to put in a fence. He said that he could put in the wire, but it was difficult for him to drive the posts. So I drove some of the posts after I got back, and did the rest of them the next morning.

The same day that I finished the post-driving job, I started back to my camp. I got to Newport, but the bus schedule wasn't too well organized, so I had to wait until the bus showed up, at about two AM the next morning. The bus depot was only open when the bus was due to arrive, so I had to wait out in the cold until then. When I finally got back to camp, I was pooped.

My log entry for March the twentieth says, "PTL, I have survived another winter."

My stepmother had given me a granny cart, and so on the fourth of April, I pushed, pulled, and dragged it to my storage unit. I found some straps in route, or I wouldn't have made it. The cart was not designed for that kind of trip. It was destroyed, but it, with the help of the straps, got the things I had loaded on it to the storage unit.

That day I checked on an apartment that looked affordable. It needed some fixing up, but I can do that sort of thing. I went to see the property management people, but they said that it wasn't ready to be rented yet.

One other thing I did that day was to retain an attorney to represent me to the Social Security Administration. After the caseworker had lost my file, I decided that I needed someone who knew the ins and outs of this system. I walked up to the State of Oregon Legal Assistance office, and the Attorney was the only one there. We talked some, and made a future appointment. The State would recover the legal fees from the Federal Government, so I didn't have to pay anything.

A few days later I had visitors again. It seems they were roaming the woods, and stumbled over my campsite. They seemed rather vague about how to get back, so I showed them where the road was.

I had left some things in Nevada in 1991, and I wanted to go get them. To this end I took a bus to Lebanon. I got there all right, and helped my father with his trailer, and a chain saw. We went out to eat and I spent the night there.

To get there I borrowed their van again. It was all the way to the Mojave Desert, a distance of over a thousand miles, one way. I went south through California, on interstate five. There was an accident on the freeway, so they routed us around it. I left the freeway just south of Mt Shasta, and didn't get back on it again until I got to Redding. I didn't know it then, but it would have been shorter to go by way of Susanville, Reno, and Las Vegas.

I took a short rest at a rest area near Firebaugh, and went on to Lost Hills, where I planned to get gas. At the gas station were some people whose pickup had broken down. It was early in the morning, and I was very tired, and some-what groggy by this time. I looked the situation over, and after checking it out, determined that the alternator had shorted out. There were no parts to be had, at that early hour of the morning, so I took them a short distance to their home. Checking that pickup out was just the thing to wake me up. If I had kept going I probably would have wrecked.

From there I drove to a rest area between Mojave, and Barstow. I rested there for several hours, and then went on to pick up my belongings. They were all still there, but the weather had gotten to some books that I had left at one place, and the rats had built a nest at the other. I sorted out the rats nest/my stuff situation with care. There could be rattlesnakes, scorpions, and tarantulas in the rat's nest. Although the rats had destroyed some of the things, I salvaged most of it.

From there I went to a location I knew about, twenty miles south of Needles, California, on Highway US ninety-five. I arrived at about two PM, and was wiped out tired.

The next day I drove down the bumpy road that I was parked on, and hiked in an area that I had been in three years before. Then I went back to my parking spot of the night before, and rested.

The Next day is Saturday, the sixteenth of April, and I'm on the road back. When I stopped for gas in Needles, I noticed a leak in the filler hose. I did some minor fixing with silicone, and went on. I got as far as about half way between Ludlow, and Newberry Springs on interstate 40, and the engine shut off.

I thought I was out of gas, but I was wrong. Anyway, I used one of the call boxes the State of California puts up along highways, and freeways, to call for help. These call boxes are a lifesaver. A tow truck came out with a can of gas, but that didn't start the van. I checked it out, and the fuel pump had quit.

As the tow truck was there, I had him load me up. We went to Newberry Springs, and he unloaded me in front of the parts house there. I didn't even go inside, I just crawled under the van, and removed the fuel pump. Surprise, surprise, they had one! In an out of the way place like this I didn't expect them to, but they did. The fact that my father's van was a Ford may have helped.

I had to get some gas at a service station to prime the carburetor, and I was on my way. I went to Barstow and stopped, as I had found other problems with the fuel system.

The van had had a custom exhaust system installed, mostly out of used parts. The people who had installed it had not done the work properly. One of the exhaust pipes blew hot exhaust gas on to the neoprene gas filler hose. The exhaust gas had damaged the hose, to the point that gas was leaking. It was a major fire hazard, to say the least.

I looked at this, and I could see that to go on in this condition was about the same as suicide. It was a Saturday, and it would be difficult, or impossible to get parts. In any case the part would be a special order item, and might take weeks to arrive. Even after I got that part of it fixed, I still needed to fix the exhaust system. Besides all this my father would need his van back a lot sooner than that.

As I was gazing at this, I noticed that the hose was a long one, and only one small section had been damaged.

So all I had to do was cut out the damaged section, and put a piece of steel tubing in the place where the damaged section of hose was. The hose was large, about two inches in diameter. I would need about three inches, in length; more tubing than the damaged area was long, so I could clamp it on with hose clamps.

Even if I got the filler hose fixed, I was still going to have to fix the exhaust system. Having hot exhaust blowing on a steel tube may not be as bad as having it blow on a hose, but it's not real good, either.

Then I had another brainstorm, I would go to a muffler shop, and get the tubing for the fuel inlet, and have them make the parts for the exhaust system as well.

This worked! There were still some problems, the muffler shop wouldn't let me work in their lot, I got the wrong size pipe for the exhaust system once, and then I had to runaround and try to adapt the parts I had had made to the old exhaust system. Then the hose from the fuel filter started to leak, and had to be replaced. All this took most of the afternoon.

On the road again, I got about half way between Barstow, and Mojave, and picked up a hitchhiker. I took him through Mojave, and dropped him off on the other side of the town. I was not going much further, at that time, and to let him off where I was going would not have been much help.

I used to hitchhike myself, and I know how much trouble it can be to be let off on the north end of a town when you are going south, or the east end of a town when you are going west. You get the idea. I used to walk for miles through some good sized towns, to get to an area that would be suitable to hitch in. Not only that, but the Police take a dim view of people hitching in their town. Some towns have laws against it, others don't, and how are you going to know? So when I pick someone up I try to let them off in a good area to hitch in, and one that will not get them in any legal trouble.

The next day I left the area I had camped/parked in

very early in the morning, and traveled all day, and some of the next night. I found a nice wrench, as I was traveling the freeway, which I still have. I stopped for the night near Myrtle Point, Oregon. (Is that where they point to Myrtle?)

I got up at about 2:30 AM the next day. I arrived at my storage unit, and unloaded the things that I had salvaged from the desert. Then the van wouldn't start! The battery was too low to turn it over. I remembered that the local Cab Company would start your car for five bucks. I called them and they came over and got me going.

I came to the conclusion that the charging system wasn't putting enough current into the battery. I would charge enough when I was driving it by day, but after a while in the dark, and the battery would be run down. I had noticed that the belts would screech right after I started the van, and had tightened the power steering belt, but this didn't solve the screeching. Now I knew what the problem was, it was the alternator belt.

First I went to the wrecking yard, and put on another alternator. No good, same problem. They let me give it back to them at no charge. Thank you! I finally came to the conclusion that the fan belt was worn out. I bought a new one, and tightened it up very tight, no more problem.

From the Coos Bay area I took the van back to my father's place, paid a visit to a friend over night, and took the bus back to my camp on the coast. Everything was all right, and no one had disturbed anything while I had been away. PTL!

There was always some concern about the security of my clothes and camping gear. It didn't amount to much, as far a value is concerned, but due to my limited financial resources it would have been a disaster to me to have to replace my things. I wear a common size in pants, and shoes, and to find these items in a thrift store doesn't happen often. I usually used two changes of clothes a week, and I had on hand enough clothes to last for several weeks.

The next few weeks were just the usual things that I had to do to survive. I had some help when I went to town to do the wash; some people picked me up, and dropped me off in town. This saved me the trouble of packing all those dirty clothes to town; all I had to do was pack the clean clothes back.

One time when I got back from town, they were having war games in the area. It was these people with their paint ball guns, and camouflage. They were hunting each other in the brush, and on a weekday too! I had to wait until they left the area before I could go to my camp.

On June the fifteenth, I got the refusal back from the Social Security people. I immediately sent the papers on to my Attorney. I knew then that it was going to be a long time before I got disability benefits from them.

My father needed some help. They burned wood at their place, and had some big oak trees, but my father was too old to do the work of cutting them down. So on the seventh of July, I got up at midnight and went to Lebanon on the bus. I was there six days, and cut down three trees, and cut them up for firewood. I visited a friend over night, and picked up a bike wheel at my old campsite near Philomath.

I didn't want to stay in the same campsite too much longer. With the mushroom pickers, paint ball warriors, and just hikers, things were way too busy around my camp. The answer was to move, and I thought I knew where.

For the last several months I had been looking at these islands in the bay. The Islands were in the east bay, and the two southern ones were overgrown, so this growth would provide good cover. Anyone would have to have a boat to get there, so they would be isolated enough. Now all I had to do was figure out a way to get there. The boat would have to be reliable, safe, and would have to fit into my storage unit as well. The boat would have to be light enough that I could carry it. Am I asking too much?

I checked with the social service agencies, and they gave their approval to the boat transportation idea. (If the boat could be considered resources, they would shut off the welfare, and food stamps.)

I finally found the prefect boat, a Kiwi Kayak. The

two-person boat was just short enough to fit into my storage unit, and with the seat out, would have enough room to put the results of my shopping, and water restocking, inside. It weighed about fifty pounds, so I could carry it. After saving up for several months, I could buy one.

What happened with all this is the subject of the next chapter.

Chapter Seven

In the previous chapter I described the process of selecting the boat, but there was still much to be done to get this all together. I had to save up enough money to buy the boat, the boat had to be ordered, and I had to locate some scrap lumber to build a shelter out of. I would need a tarp, and some nails as well. Not all the lumber I would need I could find on the beaches, so I would need some way to move plywood as well. I came up with the idea of using a truck inner tube, to load plywood, and other boards on.

To solve the first problems would just take time, so on to the next. I had to do what I could, so I walked the shoreline of the bay and the Ocean to see what I could find in the line of drift lumber. After I found it, I had to concentrate it so I didn't need to make a lot of stops to pick it up. I also had to write down where I had hid it so I could remember where it was.

In late July I had enough funds to order the boat. I ordered it in the color of olive drab green, so it would be less conspicuous. The boat was not going to be delivered until mid August, so I had some time, but I had a lot to do. My Father had given me a thick foam pad, but it was about shot. I would leave it at the mainland campsite. I went to the thrift store and bought two thin foam pads, but when I went back to pick them up, they told me that another foam pad had been donated, and if I wanted to, I could exchange it. I was glad to do it, as keeping all those layers under control would have caused me some lost sleep.

Some more work that had to be done was seeing where I could hide my food, clothes, bedding, and camping gear. I had to hide it near where I expected to pick it up. Some things I could put in buckets with lids, and stash, others I could leave out in the weather. There were some things that would have to be packed down in good weather, such as clothes and bedding. Some of the fabric things I took to the storage unit before I left.

I would need a good tide table, so I could schedule my pickups at night, when no one could see me. I also needed to check the weather before moving, or even going out on the water. When using a boat for the first time and for some time afterwards, you need to be cautious about the behavior of a boat. I was also concerned about soaking my clothes, and bedding. When I moved I put the fabric things in plastic bags for the trip.

Early in August I took some of the things I had to my storage unit. One of the reasons I was moving was that I would be much closer to everything. I could land on the bay, or Coal Bank Slough, and do whatever business I needed to. I could store the boat in the storage unit, while running errands, or visiting my Father. One other thing was because the boat was as short as it was, and didn't have a motor; I didn't have to get Coast Guard Stickers. Sounds good doesn't it. The Lord had a better idea about landing the boat! More on this later.

Part of getting ready to move was salvaging lumber. One day as I was pulling nails, near where I had the bike parked, a man showed up. He said that he had found my bike previously, and had come back to see if it was still there. By being in the area, I probably saved my bike from being stolen. I loaded the bike up the next day with some things, and rode it to the storage unit.

The same day I rode the bike to town I rented a P.O. Box. The Post Office in Coos Bay had more space, so all I had to do was wait three weeks. The box lobby was open most of the time so I could come and go on a much more flexible schedule like late at night, or early in the morning.

From the Post Office I went to see if the boat had arrived, and it had. I had stashed some boat things near the place where I bought the boat. I carried the boat about an eighth of a mile, and got ready to launch it. The first thing I did was remove the back seat. I wanted to paddle it from the front. When I launched it, I soon learned the error of my ways. I had had a rubber raft and this method worked just fine, but this wasn't a rubber raft. I got a ways, by sheer stubbornness, before I gave up and went back. The tide was well on its way out, so I had to hurry. I got the seat changed in time, and went on my way.

I went to the north shore of the bay, and landed the boat, and carried it to a place I had selected. I later learned the best way of carrying the boat, but that was a year or more a way. To carry it by holding it by the sides of the flanges was awkward and tiring.

The weekend was spent resting and packing. On Monday the fifteenth of August, I took some buckets to my stash, walked to town, and then launched the boat. I paddled down the bay, toward the entrance of the bay, where it joins the ocean. I didn't go that far, as none of my lumber piles were close to the entrance. On the way down there I paddled past a herd of sea lions. They were very smelly and noisy, and when they saw me coming some of them started for me. I immediately changed course, and they swam back to the shoal where they had their sunning spot.

To get the lumber on the boat, I had to tie it. The boat had handles cast into the plastic, which made excellent places to tie things. Some of the boards were short enough to put inside the boat, but some of them had to go on top. I made several stops to pick up my boards, and must have paddled ten miles or more, round trip. When I got back to the place that I landed the boat at, I was pooped. I took the boards off the boat, and stashed it behind a log. The tide was about high, and as it was nearly dark, I didn't think anyone would bother it.

I spent the night in my old camp. The next day, I loaded as much stuff in the boat as I could, including water jugs, food, and the lumber I had picked up yesterday and what lumber I had accumulated before. I then paddled up the bay toward the islands.

The box that I had used for a piece of luggage, and before that a cargo box on the back of a motor cycle, was now in use as a mouse proof food box. I got the measurements from the Lord, and didn't understand why it should be so important. I found out when I loaded it into the boat. It just fit through the hatch, with only a small fraction of an inch to spare. I still have it, and use it for camping trips.

I had a problem, The canoe paddle that I had did the job, but because I didn't have any skirts or covers for the kayak, it would drip water on my stuff, and me and gradually fill the boat. I had to mop out the water, and the trips I made with the boat were decidedly miserable. I finally bought a skirt for it, and made a cover for the front hatch. I didn't get this done until fall, however.

I stopped at an island I will call #3, on the way up the bay. Then I went on to Island # 1, where I planned to camp. I landed on the East Side of the Island, and had to wade in some mud, and walk through the marsh grass that grows in the tidal areas of these islands. After I got through this I had a more formidable problem, blackberries. I finally found an area of very tall grass, which got me to the dike. These Islands were the result of dredging. To do this they built a dike around the area that they wanted to fill, and filled it with what is called spoil.

I made a trail up this dike, (It was about twenty feet high.) and got over it, so I could select a location for my new camp. After I had made my selection I found a better way to enter the interior of the island. The Northwest corner of the island had a kind of short jetty, which had a short sandy beach at the end of it. I went back and got the boat, and paddled it over to the better landing area. Then I could begin the unloading process.

I still had some tide left so I went to one of the grocery stores, and the storage unit. I had left some bedding there, as well as some other items. I got back late, and tired.

The next day was Wednesday, and I still had a lot to do. The old problem of when is it going to rain, was riding me. On that day I paddled the boat up to island #3, to get some boards. I ran into a duck hunter, (It wouldn't be duck season for some month's yet.) who showed me his blind. I got my lumber, and went back to the island I was staying on. I then broke two trails, before dark. My logbook says, "Very tired."

On Thursday I started construction of my new shelter. I went out two times for boards. I had found a hand saw in the middle of the Coos Bay Bridge, in early November of last year. It cut much better that the saw that I bought at the junk shop. This just goes to show you that the Lord can supply better things than you can buy. PTL!

One time When I went to town I met a man who came to the island all the time. He had his own camp there, but lived in town most of the time. We later became friends. He too was looking for solitude.

I went on to town to pick up some things at the storage unit, and make some purchases. A department store, lumberyard combination was right in front of a body of water known as Coal Bank slough. When the tide was up far enough you could land a boat there. There was enough water to land, but the tide was on the way out, so I would have to wait to leave. This was fine by me, as I didn't want my activities to be seen anyway.

A few days earlier I had purchased a truck inner tube from one of the local tire stores. I pumped this up, and loaded four sheets of 1/2" plywood, onto it. I think I had some other boards on it as well. I had to wait until about eleven PM, when the tide came in enough to float me off, without having to wade in the mud. It took me two hours to paddle my way back to the place where I landed the boat. There was only about a mile to go, but between the tide coming in, a head wind, and the load I was towing, It was a very slow job. I also had to keep an eye out for tugs, and other waterway traffic.

To get to the storage unit I had to paddle up Coal Bank Slough, about half a mile or more to a place where there was a parking lot. I had scoped this out before buying the boat, as I didn't want to have a boat with no place to land it. I had left the boat in the storage unit, and when I went to pack it to the parking lot to launch it, some one asked if he could help. I said thanks, yes, because I hadn't yet learned to carry it by myself. We didn't have far to go, about a block or less. When I got there I loaded the boat with the things I wanted to take with me. While I was doing this, a man in the house next to the parking lot said, "Why don't you launch it from here?"

I didn't do it then as I had the boat already loaded, but after that I did. He and his wife had a salt grass lawn that sloped down to the bay, and allowed a landing at a much lower tide than was possible from the parking lot. He and I had both repaired lawn mowers, and liked to have yard sales, so as time went along we became good friends. I went to see them about once a year, and we used to exchange Christmas cards. This was what I meant when I said that the Lord had a better idea for a boat landing area. I lost contact with them late in 03.

Even with all this I still had a lot of moving to do. The Kayak was proving to be a stable and water worthy craft, but it would only hold so much. I walked back to my old camp-site, and moved my things to the top of the hill in daylight. (Packing buckets and other Items through the woods at night, is a long and hazardous undertaking.) That night I packed six loads to the bottom of the hill. The next morning I packed the last load to the bottom of the hill, on my way to town.

The lady from the Peoples Thrift place picked me up somewhere in town and helped me with this phase of my move. She had a pickup, and we also collected some of the lumber I had stashed along side the main highway. We took all this stuff to the storage unit, and unloaded it. It is now late in August, and I still haven't gotten my shelter completed.

In the next few days I covered the shelter over, and put a door in. I had gotten moved in more or less, but still needed to do things like build in a bunk, put up shelves, find a step for the front, etc. Every time I had to build something, first I had to go and hunt the lumber. This meant walking around the tidal drift areas, and walking in the deep mud between island #1 and island #2. I could go back later and tie the boards onto the Kayak, or tow them over in rafts. I couldn't walk in the mud to island #3 because there was a channel of deep water between #2 and #3.

Some where along here I discovered I needed more than reading glasses. The Oregon health plan had provisions for glasses so I got my eyes tested, and got bifocals. Old age was catching up to me; I am now fifty-one. (Actually I was fifty-one some months ago.)

On the fifth of September, I built a trail to a jetty that was not so well used as the one with the nice beach. I thought that if I had a different way to the place that people would not find me. The trail that I built was west of my shelter and about a half mile away. It was quite a job, as I had to build it through a wooded area that was also over-grown with blackberries. I got it done and then left my boat at the new dock area. I always locked the boat to a log that had a large staple driven into it. I used a covered bike chain and padlock for this purpose.

It was shortly after I had built this trail that I heard on the news that Social Security was going to speed up the processing of disability claims. I have, by this time, some idea of my problems. This was good news, as my attorney had told me that it would take about eighteen months to process my claim.

In mid September I started stocking island #2 with lumber. The intention was to build another shelter if I needed to. I always liked to keep an ace in the hole. I would stockpile some lumber, and; load it in, on, and/or tow it behind the Kayak. It was a lot of work, but it paid off later. I had a brown tarp left over from my bike repair days, and I used it to cover the lumber with.

To give you some idea of my life at this time, and for some time to come, I will share this entry from my logbook. Friday 9/23, up three AM, to North Bend. (I used the boat launch dock near the North Bend Airport for this.) To the Post Office, (In Coos Bay, I think, a distance of about four and a half miles.) three grocery stores, the eye clinic, trade books, group therapy, pay storage rent, and this is the day that I finally bought a skirt for the Kayak. All this is not in order, but you get the idea. I found a float on the way back. To get to the dock I had to paddle for about three or four miles down the bay to get there, and in the dark at that. You can't use the dock, the park, and the paved walking path anymore. It was too close to the airport, and they closed it all down in 1999.

The canoe paddle I was using would work, but I wasn't getting the speed I needed to fight the wind and tide. I went to a department store, and they had oars for small inflatable rafts. I bought a set, and took it over to the storage unit. I had found a part of a shovel handle on the beach some time before. I cut one of the aluminum tubes in two, and carved out the shovel handle so it would fit in the area between the two tube halves. This made the combined length of the two paddle blades, the tubes, and the shovel handle, about seven feet. This worked well and I used it as long as I had the boat. The carving job on the shovel handle was a real chore, as the wood was very hard, and I had to be very accurate. My Father had given me a old pocket knife, which had only two blades, but the steel was very good, and never dulled through this entire process.

I had found a three cornered file in my travels, and as I had hit a nail when building my shelter, I decided to sharpen both my saws. You have to be very careful to file only the edge that needs it. The tooth must also be filed at an angle. I must have got it right because the saw was as good as new. (When I was younger I used to cut Christmas trees, in a growers lot. I did this piecework, and as a result I learned to sharpen chain saws. Sharpening a handsaw wasn't much different.)

About every Year or so the State of Oregon's social service agencies, (It didn't matter which one your talking about.) would give you a new caseworker. On October eleventh they gave me one named William (Bill) Boose.

One problem with going back and forth by boat was that some times the tide was only high for as long as it took to get to town. Then you would be stranded on shore, until the tide got high enough to go back. This could be many hours, and hanging around a populated area with nothing to do, could attract unwanted attention. This was especially true at night. So to help with my invisibility program, I would first load the boat with water and whatever groceries I had bought, then I went to movies. I learned a lot about myself this way; one thing I learned was that I didn't like romantic movies at all. I didn't like them with sex scenes either; I found them sexually stimulating all right, but didn't like that very much. No good getting all dressed up, if you have no place to go. I tried to pick movies that were decent, but as the theaters didn't give out that kind of information, I wasn't always successful. There were other reasons that I found these movies with the sex and nudity scenes disturbing, but more on this later.

I was still learning the ropes on the boat, when in late October, I was launching the boat, I dumped it. Where I was launching it from there was a kind of stream that ran on the north side of the jetty, and out to the bay. It didn't have enough water in it to float the boat, except when the tide was coming in. Between the jetty and the bay were some marsh grass, and then the mud flats. When the tide came in, as it was when I launched the boat this time, there would be about three feet of water in the stream. I would drag the boat out to the edge of the stream, load it, and launch it. Then I would get in, rig the skirt to the hatch, and away I'd go. On the day I'm writing about the tide had filled the stream, but had not gotten into the marsh grass yet. So I pushed the boat out into the stream, but left the stern of the boat on the land. When I stepped into the boat, it immediately turned over. I was soaked to the waist. Another of life's learning experiences.

Although I had a skirt for the boat, I still didn't have a cover for the forward hatch. One of the stores in town had a sale on small tarps, so I bought one. I went to the boat and used the hatch for a pattern, but I allowed a lot of extra room around the margin. I had been finding bungee cords for years, so I took some 1/4" cords and used them for elastic. The cords I had were none of them long enough, so I crimped them together with short pieces of heavy wire. I got out my sewing kit and stitched the cover together, with the bungee cord inside. This worked for about a year, and then I had to make another one. The first one had been exposed to too much sunlight, and had deteriorated.

The next month was the usual survival stuff, buying food, back and forth to town, group and other therapy, studies of books, (I seemed to have adult children of alcoholics issues.) and other things that I did to make life interesting. I was getting a better grip on my problems all the time through my studies. There didn't seem to be any solutions, however. One thing though, because of my method of transportation, I was only able to go to the group therapy sessions about twice a month, instead of once a week.

On November the twenty eighth, I got on the bus to Newport, on the way to my Father's place in Lebanon. Somewhere there had been a problem, and the bus was forty minutes late. We got to the Newport bus station, only to find that the connecting schedule had already left. I didn't get to my Father's place till late afternoon, as a result.

The visit was one of the usual things, help around the place, or fix things they couldn't, shopping or visit friends, help friends out with their projects, and catching up on what's happening. By the second of December, I was on my way back to Coos Bay, with the usual stop over in Newport.

Once again I checked the junk shops, this time I scored. My belt was about shot, so I checked to see what they had. Some one had donated a whole rack of belts, most of them with cheap buckles. I looked through the rack and found one with a solid brass buckle. It is holding up my pants as I write this. I can't remember the price, but it was under two dollars. The buckle was worth more than that, not to mention the belt. (By 04 the belt was shot.)

I had the usual wait until the small hours of the morning, then on the bus to Coos Bay, at about four thirty A.M. I did some shopping, checked the mail, and paddled back to the island. I was very thankful to find my camp intact. I will include a passage from Psalm 4 the eighth verse; I will both lay me down in peace, and sleep: for thou, Lord, only makes me dwell in safety. I found this verse, as I was reading the entry in my logbook for this date.

I had a heavy session in group therapy on the ninth of December, and then one of the ladies at group offered to give me a ride. The Lady's mother was the driver, they had helped me once before, when I had bought the Kayak skirt. They ran me out to a large chain department store near the

Empire district of Coos Bay. I have not seen them since, but the lady made a suggestion that I later followed up on. Hope it did some good.

The end of the year found me more or less in the same state that I was in at the end of the last year. I was still hoping for the boat mission to get started, and I was waiting or a good place to rent in town. I had realized that the money that I was getting from welfare was not enough to pay any kind of rent. (I know now that I would not be able to live for very long in any apartment within my means, even on SSI.) It is now 1995.

I still thought I would get an apartment to live in, and as the money was accumulating in the bank account, I decided to spend it on something I could use. I, therefore, bought a TV and a VCR in early January.

On January ninth I failed to keep an appointment, due to bad weather. Elsewhere in this book I have made statements that I always kept my appointments, but here's where I missed. My logbook says that I didn't keep it, but it doesn't say with whom I had the appointment. I think it was with the psychologist, "P." Anyway I tried to get a hold of him, and make another appointment the next day. I made the appointment, but this time he wasn't there.

On the day after I missed my appointment, I went shopping in the junk shops and found a kayak paddle. It was about the same thing as I had made, but the tube was the right length. The Paddle blades were replaceable, so now if I broke one, I had a spare.

On the twenty third of January I was wandering about checking on things, and I ran into one of the NOOAA survey crew. They were checking on the navigational ranges on the south side of the island. It was a good day, with no bad weather in sight, so I went over to the other jetty to see the Kayak. When I got there I discovered it was gone! Somebody had broken open the log and loosened the staple. All they had to do then was slip the bike chain over the staple, and take the boat. My feelings were beyond description. How I handled this situation, and got off the island, is the subject of the next chapter.

Chapter Eight

Here I am, looking at a broken log, and no boat. When the tide gets low enough I could walk out to the east through the mud flats. This would not be a good solution. It would be a distance of a mile or more, and I would not be able to carry much. The only thing I can think of, is to get off the island, get some kind of cheap boat, get my stuff off, and go back to the camp that I was in north of North Bend.

I knew that the Coast Guard patrolled the bay in the early afternoon. I didn't think they had been through yet, so I figured to try to flag them down. My jacket had a red liner in it so all I had to do was wait where they could see me and wave the jacket. This worked, but not quite as I expected. I thought I would get a helicopter ride, but all they did on the chopper was call the buoy crew, and have them pick me up. Anyway I got to shore.

The first thing I did when I got there was call the Police. The people at a local motel let me use their phone for this, thank you again. He took down the details, but that didn't give me much hope of getting the boat back.

I walked to a department store and bought a cheap inflatable Kayak. Bad choice, it was unstable, shipped water, and presented a huge sail area to the wind. It was back to the drip from the paddle situation again. I still had the old canoe paddle, and the new one I had bought at the junk shop. I don't know which one I used, but I got the thing back to the Island. I found out all about its problems on the way.

Over the next two days I moved my things off the Island, the boat wasn't too bad when loaded, but you really had to be careful when it wasn't. In spite of the time of year there was little or no wind when I moved my things off. I can truly be thankful to God for this Grace.

The lady from people's thrift had said that if I needed help to move I should call her. I did this, only to be told that she was busy, try again in a few minutes. So I called back about fifteen minutes later, only to be told she had left. If all that keeping your word means is whenever it's convenient, I wanted no more of them. I was very angry. Someone has said, that your word is the one thing that you can both give and keep. If a person has that kind of character defect, I wanted no more to do with them. At least she could have talked to me.

My friends who docked my boat for me, had a friend who had a pickup, and after seeing whether the old camp was habitable, he helped me move back. The Lord always provides. PTL! It took five days to move off the island, check out the old place, and move back to the old camp. There is an entry in my logbook that says I got everything up the hill just before the rain started. Once again, PTL!

Because of the theft of the boat I must now walk about sixteen miles to the Post Office, where before all I had to walk was about ten. (This is round trip mileage.) On the second of February, I went to town. I was still mad about that situation with the thrift store people, so I decided to tell the person that had referred me to them, what had happened. This was "P" the therapist at the mental health clinic.

I was so mad that I really blew up. There were three reasons for my blow up, one I'm going to wait to write about. The other two are these; It takes a specially set up organization to deal with homeless people, one who has people there who can deal THEN with the individual, not whenever the organization people feel like it. The other is that if you make a promise you should be prepared to keep it. If you can't answer these statements in a positive fashion, about your organization, you are not ready to deal with homeless people.

From the mental health clinic I went on to Coos Bay. When I got there I found a note from the Officer who took the report of my stolen Kayak. It had been recovered, and there was a suspect. I called the dispatch of the Coos County Sheriff, and they made arrangements for us to get together in a grocery store parking lot. We talked about the crime, but I never knew what happened to the suspect. He told me where the boat was, and that was in North Bend.

So then I went to my storage unit and picked up the paddle, life jacket, mooring line, with the skirt, and cover. (When I was on shore talking to the Police about the theft, the day I discovered the theft, someone had stolen the first set of paddles from my campsite.) I then had to walk back to North Bend, and call the Officer responsible for found items. He was a cool dude, and we loaded the boat into his pickup, and he took me to the Bay Shore nearest the annex. I launched the boat, and paddled it back to my friend's place. My old paddles were with it. In order to conceal it's owner-ship; they had repainted it silver. I had been a beautiful day, sunny and warm. In all that day I had walked about twenty six miles, most of them carrying something, and had paddled the boat about four miles.

I had been having a pain in my guts, and went to the Doctor to see what it was. He said that it wasn't my appendix, They would have to run a test of my bowels. This test was really a pain, and they wouldn't know until the results came back what was biting me. This was late in February.

On the first of March I went to Coos Bay. I still had some stuff on the island so I went in the old Kayak and got some of it. I had to buy a scraper to get the paint off the plastic. This ruined the finish, but anything was better than that silver paint. While I was there I took care of most of the paint scraping. It was so far to walk that when I went to the Post Office, I had to do a lot of other things too.

It was time to go to see my Father again. After being stranded the last time I decided to go a different route. There was a local bus line that went to Eugene, and on to Bend. I just needed to get to Eugene; There I could get connections to Lebanon. There was some time before the next bus was called, after I got to Eugene, so I used the time to check out the local used bookstores. My Father picked me up in Corvallis, and took me to Lebanon. This was on the sixth of March.

My stepmother kept goats and chickens, and that's what I did the next day, or so says my logbook. I don't remember what I did with them, or to them.

The next day I spent shopping for books and visiting old friends. The one after that my Father and I worked on some projects in his shop, and just visited. The day after that, it was time for me to go back to the Coos Bay area.

When I got to Newport, I had the usual wait till the bus showed up in the early morning hours. I went to the junk shops as usual, and found another Christian thrift store in the process. I took in a movie, and did some shopping. Then I met the bus, and was on my way to my camp.

Even though I have just been up most of the night, I still have to go and see what's in the Post Office box. So away I go for the sixteen miles or so that I have to walk. The mushroom picker that showed up at my camp in the woods some time before, picked me up and gave me a ride, part way back. I was very tired and really appreciated it.

The next few weeks were the usual survival activities. Ducking the raindrops, buying food, looking for used books, and trying to remain invisible. I still had to walk the sixteen miles round trip to the post office.

On the tenth of April, I got a form from the Judges office. I had to fill it out to get a hearing on my claim for benefits.

It was about this time that I finally realized what my anger problem was. Some people like to be alone once in a while, but I NEEDED to be alone most of the time. To have to deal with others would, over time, provoke me to anger. The cause of this is a study in it self, but here goes.

It all started with my grandfathers, both drunks. (It probably started even further back, but I'm writing about what I know.) My Father's parents split up when he was an infant. There was no alimony, or anything like it, so my grandmother had to work. The jobs she could get didn't pay very much so she couldn't afford to pay for what passed for childcare then. (About nineteen thirteen.) So she left my Father with her parents. Both of them were elderly, and worn out by the rearing of a large family. (Eleven children.) My Father grew up feeling rejected, and rootless. This was not helped by the depression of the thirties. He married my mother about nineteen thirty-eight. My Father was an only child.

My Mother's family took a little longer to break up. My maternal grandfather was a World War One veteran. He married my grandmother after the war was over. (I think?) My mother was the eldest of three children. I have previously stated how important a fathers attention is to a girl child, well, this is where I make the application. My grandfather was a boozer, a bootlegger, and a barber. These three activities did not give him much time for the little girl who would be my mother. It didn't give him much time for his family either, for after the third child, the marriage broke up. Once again my grandmother was forced to work, but this time my Mother was there to take care of the baby sitting chores. My mother had gotten little or no positive emotional attention from her father, and now she had to be a mother to her brothers. In some ways I turned out much like my uncle, the youngest child of that family. The same person parented us. He was a loner with technical skills, and few friends.

The way it seems to work is this, if a girl doesn't get the attention she needs from her father, she expects it from her husband. This doesn't work at all, The husband, if he has had his attention needs met, can usually meet the day to day emotional needs of his wife, but not all this backlog of attention. My Father, however, had not had his needs met, and could not meet even these needs, much less the backlog of expectations that my mother had. A psychologist once told me you can't meet those past needs. I have found that to try to do so is to abuse those around you. The Bible says that God will meet all your needs in Christ Jesus. Phil 4:19 She didn't know to ask, or my situation might have been much better.

After I got to be about ten or eleven, my Mother seemed to expect something from me, but she would never tell me what it was. When I was about twelve I was told to do something, (I can't remember what.) and when I had completed the work, my Mother seemed to want something more. I asked her, "What do you want?" "You know." She replied. I didn't have a clue. I finally figured it out when I was about fifty. She wanted some emotional attention. She was trying to replace the missing parts of her childhood. I have said before that if you don't give a child some emotional attention when they are young, they won't have any to give when you are old. She didn't know all this, and it wasn't her fault anyway. The result to myself was devastating, however. I think she tried to manipulate me to meet her attention needs. She used to tell me I was being selfish, this hurt, and I still didn't know what she wanted. If you manipulate some one, you've abused them. (Some of these places that have a lot of office politics are abusive too. I think that is why you have these office shootings. You can abuse people beyond conscience.)

I was emotionally neglected on one hand, and subjected to emotional demands on the other. Do you know how it feels to have emotional demands made on you; demands you haven't got the resources meet? You feel like your being mugged. In self-defense I learned not to have feelings.

I tried to meet my needs for attention at school, with the result that the other children saw me as vulnerable. I was pounded, ran ragged, and generally hassled. When I tried to do something about it, I was a bad kid. None of the teachers did anything to stop the abuse. I still have no use for the educational system. To me it's a sort of a free form child abuse. It's not surprising to me when I hear of some child who has killed his teachers, and classmates.

One other thing my Mother used to do to meet her attention needs was pick a fight with my Father. This was traumatic to me. If a child is traumatized, the trauma can stop, or stunt a child's emotional growth. It took a while to figure out, but I think my growth stopped at about the age of twelve. The only way you can help the situation is to get all the feelings out in the open. Unfortunately that won't work for me, because that puts an emotional demand on me. If you put an emotional demand on me, sooner or later you get a blowup, like the one with the psychologist, "P."

My parents did the best they could with me. Considering the problem homes they came from, it's something of a miracle that I turned out as well as I did. I'm sure they cared about me, they just didn't have the capacity to adequately care for me. They didn't know this though, and there was no one to tell them.

I used to run away from home a lot with the result that I got into some minor scrapes with the Law. They finally put me in the State Hospital. The problem with that was that they wanted to make me like everyone else. This wasn't going to work, because they completely ignored my emotional development. The result is that through most of my adult life I've been split. On one hand I wanted to be like others, and live a reasonable life. On the other I needed to be alone. What should have been done, is to find out what kind of a person I was, and help me to find work situations I could cope with. This all happened when I was sixteen.

In the process to survive all this I lost, or never developed some feelings that others have. The result of this is when some one makes an emotionally loaded statement to me; I may understand part of the emotions, or none of them. I usually react to the definition of the words-sentence. Even though I have a very good vocabulary, and when the Clinical Psychologist tested me I got 100% on the vocabulary test, I still do not understand everything that is said to me. It's like being partially blind; there is some perspective I don't have. (I recently had a problem with a man in the place where I live. He said I don't listen.) I just don't hear the emotions, or relate to them.

In the process of my studies I learned something about stress. It seems that the human body only puts out so much adrenalin in a person's lifetime. Once that is gone you don't handle stress very well. I think, that because of all the hassles of growing up, I used up most of my allotment by the time I was twenty. The result of this is that I don't like excitement. I like to be busy, amused, interested, or bored.

This desire to be unexcited carries over to sex as well. Coupled with the fact of my emotional immaturity, makes it very unlikely that I would make much of a partner. The emotional demands of a normal marriage would be too much for me as well. The nicest, most attractive, easiest to get along with woman in the world, and I would leave in about three weeks. I would probably do better with one that

100

wasn't so attractive, but the emotional demands would more than I could bear.

I know that the Bible says that God can sort all this out, but it also says you don't want to tempt him either! Anyway I've decided to be myself in Christ Jesus, and let Him put as much of Himself in me as I can hold. I know that God makes people for his own purpose, and it is possible that writing this book to explain the process of becoming emotionally disabled, and how it feels to be homeless, may be one of His purposes for me.

When I finally realized all this, I also realized that the boat mission was not for me. If I could not cope with normal emotional demands in the work place, I had no business being cooped up with several people in the relatively small area a sailboat would provide. This was also the reason the Lord did not provide the funds to buy said sailboat. I wasn't the right person. If I had not gone in that direction though, I never would have figured all this out.

It is now time I moved back to the island, it's late in April, the worst of the bad weather is over, and I still don't like to walk the sixteen miles round trip to the Post Office. On the twentieth of April I packed up to leave. I didn't bring all the stuff I usually have so that makes it a little easier. The next day I got up at two AM, and packed four loads to the stash area near the landing site. Then I took the bike to the bottom of the hill. I took a break, then I biked to town where I washed the clothes. Then I went on to three grocery stores, and the Post Office. From there I went to the storage unit, and got out the boat, loaded it, and paddled it out to the island. I checked the camp out and everything is OK. PTL!

I then unloaded the boat, and paddled to the landing area, near where I stashed my things. I have arrived at about 10:30 PM. I went to the old campsite, and packed out one load. Then I built a fire on the beach and waited for the tide to come back in. The next day the tide is in about 3:30 A.M., and I can paddle my way to the island I've been camping on. I'm very tired, but I still have to unload, and organize my camp, plus I'm very dirty after a night on the beach, so I took a spit bath.

Chapter Nine

I don't think I've described the spit bath, so here goes. You need a small bucket; and a place to stand as you are washing that will not get your feet dirty after you've washed them. You also need privacy, a bar of soap, a sponge, and a towel. You take the bucket and fill it with about a quart of water. Then you strip down, and wet the sponge. You take the bar of soap and rub it around on the sponge until the sponge is completely saturated with soap. You then scrub yourself all over, from your neck to your feet. Then you wash your head by getting it wet, and scrubbing it with the soap. You then rinse off by dumping the remaining water over your head. You will probably need to reload the sponge several times in this process. This is not going to get the entire job done, but it's better than nothing. This process is very interesting, not to mention chilly, in cold weather. In order to clean up this way in cold weather, a heat source needs to be immediately available, or start walking or other exercise. If you don't, you could wind up with hypothermia, which could be fatal.

It is now late April of 1995, and I still have some things to move from the stash area to the island. So the day after I got back to the island, away I go again. I got there all right, but after I got there the wind came up. It was a nice sunny day except for that cold north wind. The only problem was, in order to get back; I had to go at right angles to the wind. This could be bad, because I didn't know whether I could keep the boat under control or not. I loaded the boat and kept as close to a dock as I could, to shelter myself from the wind.

A tug was pushing a ship onto the dock, and I came right behind his stern. After the water has been churned up like that, the paddles don't bite the same. The water feels loose, or something.

After I got beyond the dock, I was right in the path of

the wind, but the boat was loaded heavy enough that I didn't loose control. The bay was chopping up pretty good by then, and water was washing over the boat in front of me, but the skirt, and cover kept it all out. The rest of the trip was uneventful, except after I got to the east bay I had a tail wind. The tail wind made the paddling easier.

On May the sixth, I went to island # 2 to see how my boards were doing. I also did some beach combing, on the island I was on. I didn't take the Kayak; I wore an old pair of shoes, and waded in the mud between the islands.

I was starting to work on one area of my problems at this time. Neither of my parents drank, when I was a child, but because my grandfathers were alcoholics, I had adult children of alcoholic's issues. This was something I could work on by myself. It seems that it is the attitudes that are passed on to the children. I had some of these attitudes. My sister had them too, and finally died of substance abuse.

The reason some people with adult children of alcoholic's issues marry each other, is that these are the people they feel comfortable with. My attitudes and your attitudes agree. Except for the Grace of God these marriages will result in a nonfunctional family, and messed up kids.

My island has some problems, mosquitoes, and hay fever. I can deal with the mosquitoes, but not the hay fever. This is one of the reasons I came to the coast, to get away from the hay fever. I have found that I have a reaction to over the counter allergy medication. On the back of the medication are some warnings. Among them it says something like, "May cause irritability, especially in children." In me too, I finally had to quit taking them before I killed someone. I wouldn't be at all surprised to find out that people have been killed, when some one else has been taking these pills. I am hoping that I will get disability soon, so I tough it out.

Another project I've decided to do, is a study of Elijah, and John The Baptist. It seems that both had a message of turning from sin to God. In a lot of ways their lives were like mine, at least as far as their lifestyles were concerned.

On the nineteenth of May, I find I may have a hearing with the Social Security Judge. This is good news, now maybe I can get off the street. There is going to be a lot more to it than that, as I will eventually discover. This hearing is probably going to be in July.

On June the second, my friends, where I docked the boat, were having a yard sale. I helped them and sold some of my stuff too. This included the inflatable Kayak. In all I took in $53.30. I also had some more room in the storage unit. The second day wasn't so good, $1.70. It hadn't rained in a while, but the day after the sale it did. I was thankful that we got the sale in before it rained.

Periodically the state does a recheck of your disability; they call it a reassessment. I had an appointment with a clinical psychologist. It was on June twelfth. This time Mr. Boose wanted me to go to a different one. He said he was a nice guy, and wouldn't give me a hassle. So, at the appointed time I arrived, and did the interview. One of the things that were discussed was possible employment. I told them that I thought I could stuff envelopes, and possibly temporary work. To work with others would be impossible, due to my lack of emotional capacity. This was to have some interesting side effects, and worked out to my benefit, but it would be years before I realized it.

On the twentieth of June, I was informed by the Senior and Disabled Services, of the State of Oregon, That my benefits would be terminated in the fall, and would be reduced by about $37.00 immediately. The State workers had had a strike, and it looked as if this was where they were going to get the money to give them a raise.

I called up Mr. Boose and asked him what had happened. He said that the rules had changed, and I was no longer disabled. Of course they wouldn't tell me what the new rules were, before the appointment, I might have been able to make the system work for me!

To say I was mad would be a lie, I was furious. I felt that my trust had been betrayed, I had been manipulated by this new psychologists questions. (And thereby abused!) He was nice about it but no mater how nice you are about it if you abuse someone it's still abuse. It was obvious that the new man was a tool in all this, and that is why they used him. I also felt that this was going to make it difficult, or impossible to get disability Social Security. It took two months to find me emotionally disabled. It only took eight days to cancel the finding.

I was so mad that I sent the food coupons and check back to the Senior and Disabled Services and went to the Social Security office, and canceled the impending hearing. I felt that if I saw the Judge in my state of mind I would probably try to kill him. I didn't care then whether I ever heard of these people again. The Lord was working in my behalf in all this, as will be seen.

That day I found some people to sell off the things in my storage unit to, and get loose from that responsibility. A lot would have to be done, some would be sold to second hand stores, some would be donated to thrift stores, some would be junked, and some would have to go to the island. At this point I had no hope of ever getting off the street. I didn't sell anything at this time, however.

Even though I had no hope of getting off the street, I was going to do what I could to see if I could find a way to make a living. I called my friends who had let me use their garage to fix the pinto, and asked them if I could use their place to receive the material to stuff envelopes, and use their location temporarily to stuff them, but the answer was no way. I made four calls to a local mission, ditto results. I would rent the storage unit for another month or so. I would have a place to stuff them, If I could get someone to receive them for me. In the process I was hauling things to the island, and sometimes making two or more trips a day.

I made an appointment at Community Action, to see the Director of Housing and Homeless Services. (I think I got the title right!) A few days later, on the twenty sixth of June, I had an interview with the man. He gave the OK to the plan, they would receive the material, I would haul it to the storage unit in a cab, and I could stuff the envelopes there, and mail them at the Post Office. One thing he told me was to check these businesses out with the Better Business

Bureau.

The local library had typewriters in it that you could use, so I wrote seven letters on them, to companies that advertised for people to stuff envelopes, and mailed them. They all wanted stamped self-addressed envelopes, so I had to get some large envelopes to put all this in.

On the twenty eighth of June, I took a bus to Portland, Oregon. I took a city bus from the bus depot, out Interstate Avenue in north Portland. I walked back toward the city center, on Interstate, from Columbia Blvd. I was distributing Gospel tracts, and leaving them in bus shelters. I got all the way back up Interstate, and was waiting for a bus myself, when a lady got off a bus and went into a shelter, She walked by me a minute or so later, with one of my tracts in her hand. PTL! (I've used this PTL all through this book. For those that don't know, this means Praise The Lord.)

From Portland I took the bus to Albany, where my Father picked me up, and took me to his place. The next day was spent putting up wood for the winter, for my Father and my stepmother. On to Eugene the next day, where I lost my tickets, and found them again, for which I was thankful. I continued on that day to Coos Bay. I did some shopping, and kayaked my way to the island. Nobody had bothered anything. PTL!

Every year the City of Coos Bay puts on a firework display on the fourth of July, so the other solitude seeker and I decided to watch. The jetty that we landed on was handy to watch from, the only problem was the mosquitoes. We both had repellent to put on so it wasn't too bad. They made a nice show, but it was kind of cold watching.

When I went to town on the fifth of July, I thought to check with the postal supervisor, about bulk mailings. He too advised me to check with the Better Business Bureau.

I had received some of my envelopes back, and the material that I got on the stuffing job sounded good. Too Good! One company would pay me three dollars each envelope to stuff their letters. Let's all quit our jobs and stuff envelopes for a living! Down in the corner it said that you have to do it exactly as they say. Well, that makes sense, your employer is going to want a good job done.

One company was based in Austin, Texas, so I called the Better Business Bureau there. They played two recordings for me; the first was either attributed to the postal inspectors, or directly from them. The first one said something like this; nobody makes money, stuffing envelopes. The legitimate, (And that's the word they used.) outfits stuff by machine. The U. S. Postal Inspectors have shut down about one thousand, (It could have been twelve hundred.) of these operations in a twelve month period.

The second recording said that the company that I was inquiring about has a lot of unanswered complaints. I think that nobody could do it quite good enough to get paid. Until I left the Postal box, I got the most junk mail that anyone had ever heard of. There were pyramid schemes, advertisements for lists of gullible people, to send them to, and get rich quick schemes, some of them legal, and most of them not. Most of them I either used for scratch paper, or just trashed. One of them was so obviously illegal, that I turned it into the Post Office people. So much for the envelope stuffing job.

One more word about this deal; I was going through Newport, on my way over to see my Father, and as I had some spare time, so I thought I would check one of these places out. The address was in Newport. I found the street all right, but no house number. What's going on here? There was a motel nearby, so I asked there, and was told that someone had tried to find them too. They wanted to reposes a car! The only way they could make this work, is to put up a mailbox in front of a vacant lot. This would only work until the Postal Service got wise, probably not very long. The old saying that if it sounds to good to be true, it probably is, certainly applied here. Between envelopes, postage, telephone calls, and etcetera, I had spent about twenty dollars to find this out.

There was one more thing I wanted to try, and that would not be full time work, but would keep me busy part of the year, and give me some cash for the rest of the year. I don't know whether I did this before or after I tried the other deal or not. This was firewatcher for the State forestry. To do this I had to have a resume. There followed my first experience with computers. (Guess what? A computer is not a typewriter!) In two or three sessions, with a lot of help from the gals in the library, I got a document that would pass muster. They had to take your application at the forestry place, but the only people that got hired were forestry students, as I later learned.

On July the sixteenth I smelled some thing bad. The local rat population had decided to make a nest under the wooden box that I used for a front step. Phew! I killed the small ones, but the mom got away.

I had heard about vocational rehabilitation, so I made an appointment with them. We talked a lot, and they said they would call and leave a message. (Community Action would take messages for you, if you were trying to get work.) They never called.

On the twentieth of July, I went to town, shuffled things around in my storage unit, and paid the rent on it. In the process I walked all over town trying to get work. I went to the State Employment Agency, a thrift store, and an operation that would train you as an over the road tractor trailer driver. This last sounded like a good deal, and it was funded by a federal grant, so no cost to me. After going through the process of interviews, and group presentation, the grant ran out and the program was canceled. This took a matter of weeks.

On August ninth, I came down sick. I had a fever, and was very weak. For two nights I went through the process of fever, breaking fever, once a night. On the eleventh I decided to see a Doctor, so I paddled to shore, but was so weak that I couldn't walk very far. The clinic was up on the hill, and I knew I wouldn't make up, so I called a cab. The Doctor diagnosed me a having an infection, and gave me some antibiotics. It was all down hill, so I could walk back.

The next Monday, the fourteenth I had an appoint-ment with the Doctor again, but was much better. He gave me some more pills, and I made a full recovery.

I could see that I wasn't going to get anywhere with the job search, and because I didn't have money to last forever, I decided to follow up on getting rid of the things in the storage unit. So On August the twenty fifth, I met a man from one of the local second hand stores at my storage unit and sold some of my tools, my bike, and a brand new thirteen-inch TV. It wasn't so much pain as you might expect, but it still didn't feel good having to give up my dream of getting off the street. Three days later, my friend with the pickup and I took a lot of furniture to a thrift store in the area. When I got back from that I trashed what was left, swept out the storage unit, and called the landlord and told him it was empty. The problem with this was that I now had, in my camp, a whole lot more things than I really wanted. That was the way it would be for awhile.

I didn't like the place I was in for several reasons, hay fever, too many people knew about me there, and to maintain my invisibility, I decided to move. Once again I waited until after Labor Day to start the process. This will start the next chapter.

Chapter Ten

On Labor Day of 1995, I sharpened my brush knife, and hand saw. To sharpen the hand saw I used a three cornered file that I had found. You had to be careful to sharpen only the right edge, and not to file anything else. This was the first step to moving.

On the fifth of September I went to the island that I wanted to move to, that is island #2, to check on the boards I had stashed there. In the process I walked around the island, to look for more building material. I found a wheel, with a tire on it. This wheel would come in handy when I went to build a stove. I went back to the island I was camping on and checked to see if the lumber that I had found there was still there, and it was.

The next day I went to town, and asked at one of lube shops for a grease barrel. These barrels are of fifteen-gallon capacity, and would fit in the Kayak. I picked up the barrel a few days later. I also bought some nails on this trip. As I recall, I found the rest of the lumber I needed on the islands. Thank you Lord!

The seventh of September, I picked up the lumber I had found the day before. There were two 14 foot 4" by 6" beams, and two 12 foot 2" by 4" boards. They were too big to tie on top of the boat, so I tied them together, and towed them behind the boat. I got there all right, and packed the 4" by 6" one at a time to the place I had picked for a camp area. As I recall, it really worked me to get them moved. These timbers would be the foundation for my new shelter. I then cleared the area I wanted to build in.

I had found some stove pipe right after I got to the Coos Bay area, and had stashed it under my first shelter, so I went to the area in the Kayak, and picked it up. It was one length of stovepipe, and an elbow. The tides didn't work to well for me, so I didn't get back till about midnight. This was on the eighth of September.

I rested the weekend, and on Monday went to my new campsite, and went to work. I put in the floor that day, and got four rafters up. This shelter was going to be bigger. Instead of eight foot by eight foot, it was going to be eight foot by twelve foot. The reason that I wanted it to be bigger, was the stove. I didn't want to start a fire by having it too close to the walls. I was hindered in my efforts by mosquitoes and bumblebees.

One reason for selecting this island was that it was more of a plateau. The one I had been on had a dike, but it had never been filled in. The result was a moist bottom area that retained its water. This grew the plants that caused me allergic trouble. The new location would dry out quickly, and cause me little or no problem.

On the twelfth of September, I finished the rafters, fit the door, put the plywood on the front end, built the bed, and installed the tarp. Once again my log said, "Very tired." At least this time I didn't have the time constraints that I usually did, as I already had a shelter.

The next day I went to town, and checked out the work scene. The State Employment Service had a referral for me, but I had to act fast! A delivery company wanted a driver to go back and forth to Eugene. To get the job you had to get a drivers record from the Department of Motor Vehicles. They wanted it that day, in Eugene. To get it I would have to get the report from the Motor Vehicle people that day, and fax it to Eugene.

I went to the Motor Vehicles Department, and paid my three dollars, but didn't ever receive the report for which I paid. I faxed what I had to the company, but pointed out that the State of Oregon wasn't interested in now, it was whenever they got around to it. This was one job I probably could have done, if I could have gotten the cooperation of the State of Oregon. I never heard anything from my potential employer.

That was the day I hung the door on my new shelter. (No, I didn't use any rope to hang the door.) I was, by now, camping in my new shelter, but I had a lot of things to move.

I made two trips the next day, one in the morning early and one late in the day. As this was not a long distance to paddle, the only problem was to pack the things to the landing sites, and then pack them to the place where I was camping. This was quite a chore, about an eighth of a mile to the jetty landing, and about a quarter of a mile to the new camp. The Kayak could carry more than I could, so I usually stashed some of it, and came back for it later.

I had finally come up with a way to carry the Kayak. First I put on the daypack, with all the things I needed to operate the boat in it. (Mooring line, flash light, and some other gear.) Then I put on the life jacket. I would then stand the boat on the stern end, and back up to it. I would hook the collar of the life jacket in the front of the rear hatch. Then I could stand up straight, tilt the boat forward at an angle of about forty-five degrees, and away I went. I could carry the Kayak the quarter of a mile I had to travel, with turns and small changes in the ground, without strain. I usually made at least one more trip to get the paddle, and any other cargo I might need.

Right across the bay, about a half a mile or less, was a good place to land the boat. It had a nice little beach, and was ideal. I talked to the businesses to either side of it and got the OK. I had told them that I would be coming and going with the tide, and so would keep strange hours. One of the businesses told me I could chain the boat up to their back fence. PTL! There was a service station nearby where I could get water, so I had improved my survivability.

On the sixteenth of September, I built the stove, among other things. To build a barrel stove, you have to have a place for the smoke to go out, a place to put fuel in, and some holes down low for a draft. I had the cold chisel that I found in the road some years before, so I got started.

The first job was the trickiest, to cut out the hole for the stovepipe. I set the end of the pipe on the location where I wanted it, and made a circle around it, on the metal. Then, starting in the center of the circle, I made pie shaped wedges in the metal, using the cold chisel, and a hammer.

After completing this process, I bent the pie shaped pieces up, until the stovepipe would fit snugly over them.

The next thing was the door to the hearth area. To do this you have to have room below the door for ashes, and the draft holes. As I recall I left about six inches from the bottom of the door to the bottom of the barrel. I wanted to use the metal I cut out for a door as well, so that meant a straight edge on the hinge side. I made my marks and started cutting, then straightened the edges, so I would have a reasonable fit. I had a hand drill in my tool kit, and used this to drill holes to bolt the hinges on. To do this you put the hinges on the door, then mark the places where the bolts have to go in the body of the stove. You always want to hold it a little high to compensate for sag.

I only punched a few holes in the front of the barrel for draft, as I didn't know how much would be needed. I could put in more holes later, but it was difficult to plug them up again after you've made them! I set the stove on the old wheel I had found, and I had to cut the tire off it when it got too hot. The stovepipe I had found was not enough to do the job, so I bought an elbow, and two lengths of pipe. The pipe went up for two lengths, out one length, and then up again once the smoke got outside. I used some wire to suspend the pipe, as it went through the hole and after it got outside. I used some tin to plug the hole where the pipe went through.

Now that I've got my stove, I need some wood, and a woodshed to keep it dry in. On the twentieth of September, I built the woodshed out of leftover material from the shelter. It was about seven feet long, four feet wide, and five feet high. I roofed it with a piece of leftover tarp from my bike repair days. Not very big is it? I only planned to use the stove in the evening, or when it was too foggy, or when it was storming. It would turn out that I used it a lot in the morning too. That way no one would notice the smoke. Therefore I didn't need too much wood.

The twentieth was also the day that I finished moving in to my new camp. I was now fifty-two years old. I have been on the street for over five years now.

The next day I start packing wood, it is a hot day. I have a lot to do to get the wood in for the winter. To do this I have a small double bitted axe, and I take two buckets with me. Because the stove is small I can only use wood if it is about eight inches long, and not very big around. This makes for a quick fire, but one that has to be continually tended. So I went to the drift areas of the island, and picked up small stuff, and I chopped up that which was too big. Better to do it now when the weather is good, than have to do it when it's pouring. Although my woodshed is not large it will take quite a few trips to fill it. There was plenty of dry wood, and several junk shake bolts. The old shake bolts were of cedar, and would make good kindling.

Two days after I moved in and I had visitors, a man and his two sons. You always wonder if the next visitor you have will be the Police. Not this time.

On the twenty eighth of September, I went to North Bend to take advantage of an add they had in the paper. It was for a transistor radio with a weather channel. There was, (And maybe still is.) a NOAA weather broadcast station in the Coos Bay area. I could now get accurate, up to date, forecasts, which I needed to plan my activities, especially my boating activities. I still have it and it still works. I use it for camping trips now.

I was having rat problems again, this time they were getting in. There were two things I needed to do about this, stop the rat highway, and kill the rats. The first was easy, but I knew that they would eventually chew their way in if I didn't do something about them. They could smell food! I went to town on the sixth of October, and in the process, I bought two rattraps. I baited them as I had the mousetraps, and caught a rat the first night. I caught three or four in all, and never had any more problems.

The five-gallon bucket was the handiest thing; you could put all kinds of things in one. I was always finding them on the beach, floating around, and I found one, that I still have, in the mudflats north of island #2. The bail was rusted out, I had to clean off the barnacles, I had to find a lid, but I've gotten a lot of use out of it.

I didn't pick up cans all the time I was homeless, it was too conspicuous, and I didn't need the money anyway. Out on the islands was a different matter, there was no one handy to see me, and there weren't enough of them to cause a scene when I turned them in anyway. I don't drink, so I didn't collect any alcoholic beverage containers. The main reason for picking them up is to recycle them.

On the ninth of October I typed and sent some jokes I had invented to the Readers Digest magazine. I thought they might get me some money, anyway it was worth a try. I have done this since, with other subject mater as well, with the result that it took a year and a half to get a rejection slip. I didn't get anything back, no jokes, no articles, no rejection slip, nothing from Readers Digest. I have concluded that this is not a good way to make money. They seem to think something for nothing is a good deal. So I am here going on record to say that it isn't. I hope that this reduces their revenue of the fruit of other people's ideas to nothing, and so puts them out of business.

The stove worked well, but until the paint burned off it was a bad scene. It smoked me out the first few times I lit it off. The wood was in before the rains started, for which I was thankful.

I had been stocking up the place for the winter. This required a lot of paddling, and quite a bit of planning. The process took over a month, but was a needed part of my survival program. You never knew when you might have a run of bad weather, be crippled, sick, or someone steals the boat again and strands you. I had a lot of water as well, for the same reasons. I was finished with this process on the twenty sixth of October.

There were a lot of broom bushes on the islands, and I had a gap in my concealment. Therefore I got some small bushes, and transplanted them. When they got big they would help to hide my shelter.

The weather got colder in November, we had frost. When you have to go out in the Kayak, and it's frosty, The first few minutes hurt. The cold hurts right into your chest. You just keep on, though, and you'll get warmed up. You had a choice, either cold weather, or stormy. I'll take the cold. At least I wasn't being blown all over the bay. I finally got smart and put some soggy wood in the boat for ballast when I had to go out in windy weather.

The other problem when it's cold is fog. I've seen it so foggy at night, that I couldn't see my destination. I knew in which direction it was, but between the darkness and fog, it didn't exist. I would start paddling in the direction I knew it to be in, and gradually there would be a vague glow from the lights. I would head for this and arrive at my destination. I was always concerned about traffic in the channels because they couldn't see me. Therefore I had to see them first, or hear them, and stay out of the way. I nearly got run down one night when a dredge that was stopped started moving, but made it OK.

On December the twelfth, a bad storm came though. The shelter jumped with every gust, but didn't move. After it was over I had to fix the tarp where it had chaffed against the wood. To do this you need some silicone sealant material, and some duct tape. You squirt the silicone on the duct tape, and apply it to the damaged area. You do this on both the inside and outside of the hole, making a tarp sandwich. I used cardboard to prevent any more chaffing.

After a storm, all kinds of things would drift in. When the weather settled down I would go beach combing, on all the islands. I was stocking up on lumber again, mostly just locating it for future reference. You never know when you might have to relocate. If you do, then having the material handy to build another shelter, could be a major factor in my survival. The next few weeks were occupied with this salvage operation, when the weather was good.

On the day after Christmas, I went to shore, and walked north to the Hauser area. I needed the exercise, and I found some things I could use. I had walked about eight-een miles, what with shopping, and just walking.

What I hope to accomplish in 1996;

1) A different life style, a little more like every one else!

2) Children books (Books on the problems children have.) plus studies on relationships.

3) Start reading the Christian books under bed, in a box.

On the second of January of 1996, I went to town, and did some shopping. Some showers landed on me on the way back, but when I got to the landing area, they quit. I got unloaded in the dry, for which I'm thankful.

On the eighth of January, I went to another island to salvage some lumber, and bring it back. I made two trips with the lumber, and then I went back for a big spool that had washed in. This spool was of the kind the Power Company uses to store wire on. Some one had used it for lawn furniture, and had put on a piece of plywood for a top. They had also painted it brick red. I had found it some days before, and thought about pushing it across through the mud, but decided that the process would be too much for me.

I rolled it out to where I could tow it, but it was a very slow job. The thing was very awkward, and it was no better when I went to tow it. It would have made an excellent sea anchor. I wanted it for the same reason that the people that painted it did, lawn furniture. After I got it to the landing area, I still had to get it to my camp. I was tired, by this time, so I just left it where it wouldn't drift away. My log says that I had a good day.

On January the eleventh, I walked to my old camp north of Coos Bay. I was keeping my options open, if I got told to leave one place; I could go back to one of my previous camps. Some time before this I had checked on my camp on the other island, but it would need a new tarp before it could be used again. The one north of Coos Bay didn't need a tarp, because it was under the trees. The trees sheltered the tarp from the Sun, so it lasted longer.

The seventeenth of January, I went to town and bought a daypack, When I got back I found the spool, that I had towed over, had been moved to the end of the jetty. I usually landed in the middle of the jetty, because that was closer to my camp. I figured that someone was going to come back for it, and I'd better move fast if I wanted it. So after my trip to town, I got busy and rolled this monstrosity all the way to camp. I never used it much, so I guess I should have let them have it.

I had found a plastic garbage can lid on the island, and as I was walking around town, I found a plastic garbage can. The last thing I did in town on the last day in January, was pack this garbage can back to the boat. It was about half a mile or so. When I got it back, lo and behold, the lid I had found fit! It was filthy, and I had to clean it, but it came in handy when I moved off the island.

On the first of February I went to town to notify the Police about a boat I had found. It had drifted in to the island I had camped on at the first. I had to tell them two times in all, and I had to move it to where they could see it. It was heavier that the Kayak, but I got it on my back, and staggered to a place where they could find it. The mooring line was rotten, and when there was a storm, it had broken. I hope they got it back all right.

On the fifth through the eighth of February, it stormed, and I couldn't go anywhere. It was a good thing I was prepared for this, and had stocked up. I only went to town once that week, as a result of the weather. The rest of the time I just tried to stay warm. Once again the camp stove came in handy, as well as the barrel stove.

On the tenth of February, I went beach combing again. I thought that after all those storms I would find a lot, but mostly what I found were pop cans.

The thirteenth of February was a good day for shopping, so I went to town. I went to seven grocery stores, got my hair cut, and visited three used bookstores, and bought some jeans at Wal-Mart. I found two straps, some change, and a cold chisel. It was going to be late before the tide would be in, so I took in a movie, as well. How far I had walked I don't know, but it was probably more than ten miles. My logbook says that the next day was spent sorting out my purchases.

I don't like being negative, but here go. I remember this well, and my logbook gives me some details that I had forgotten. I was still continuing my studies, and had started a book, when I discovered something that made me junk the book.

It seems that this man came to the author for counseling, but the shrink, (I can't remember whether he was a Psychologist, or a Psychiatrist.) wouldn't tell the man what was wrong with him. What's wrong with this picture? After all the man had paid to find out what his problems were. In the book the shrink had said something like, "but of course I couldn't tell him." What's this "of course" garbage?

The only thing that makes any sense, is that the shrink was afraid that the man would do harm to himself. Of course, he might have gotten his life together too! The only conclusion that I can come to is, that these people of the psychological profession, because of their education, think they can play god. My great grandfather fought in the Civil War, on the side of the north, So that people that didn't have a choice could have one. I will grant you that not all their choices have been good, BUT that doesn't mean that they shouldn't have the right to make them. If you take away the right to choose, you have depersonalized a human being. If you have depersonalized a human being you have abused them. Some rights we should not have, to maintain good order in society, but to pay for services or a product, and not receive it is a fraud.

I know that the right to have an abortion is not one of those rights we should have, but I think that the way that the protest movement is handling the situation is not good either. I think the way to deal with this is to discern what needs the individual is trying to fulfill by their behavior and show the individual who is contemplating a abortion how she might better fulfill those needs. To just say "you are wrong," is judgmental. The Bible says," Judge not, that ye be not judged." Mathew 7:1. The way they feel is that you are not allowing them to choose, and so they can't fulfill their needs.

On the twentieth of February, I went to town on one of my shopping trips, but when I got ready to go back, it had started to blow. I made it all right, but the wind was so strong that I couldn't carry the boat back. I stashed the Kayak, and some of my supplies, and got back as quick as I could. I had already had a shower on the way back, and that was just the beginning of the storm. I went back the next day and got the boat and supplies.

The first of March found me cleaning the rat's nest out of the wood shed. As I burned the fuel I worked from one end of the shed to the other. I finally got enough room to clean out the rat's nest.

I didn't know that geese nested so early. I had discovered the goose on a nest, on and island that I called Two Bush Island. This was on the eighth of March. After this I would curtail my explorations so I didn't disturb the nesting birds.

Once again I have an appointment for a Social Security hearing, with a Judge. It's on April nineteenth. As it doesn't look like anything else is going to happen, this is it. I got the notification on March the twenty eighth. When I got the notification, I just looked at it for a long moment, and I nearly threw it in the trash. I didn't though, and I let them know that I would be there. I had no feeling whatsoever about trashing the thing, or responding. Curious.

On April one, I wrote a synopsis of my problems, which I have already given some account of. I Think I have these notes, but I have tried to give this information in this book as I either learned it, or developed it.

On the fourth of April I got a letter from my Attorney about the coming hearing. I made a call, and set up an appointment for the next Thursday. (This was Tuesday.) The deal was for the Attorney to pick me up where I landed the boat.

The next Thursday the Attorney was there, and so was I. We went to a mall, and looked over the paperwork, and discussed the situation. The results looked good. Now all I had to do was survive until the hearing. This is part of what will be discussed in the next chapter.

Chapter Eleven

It was raining early in the morning of April nineteenth, when I paddled the boat to the landing near the businesses. I walked to the down town area, and hung out for a while, until businesses started opening their doors. I didn't like to hang out very much, as the Police could be very curious about such behavior. The Lord was with me, and nobody noticed and called the Police.

My hearing isn't until early afternoon, so I walked around town, and grocery shopped. I was in six stores, my logbook says.

They had the hearing in the BLM Ranger station, and office building. I got there early, and ate my lunch, which I had bought, at a grocery store. I often ate chef salads, as that was part of my Doctors orders, for my intestinal condition.

My Attorney came for me and took me into the hearing room. I was asked to identify myself into a microphone. Then the Judge made a statement, it went something like this, "If I would drop my claim for workmen's disability, he would grant my claim for Supplemental Security income." (When I had made my claim in late 1993, I had made a claim for both.)

The Judge then told us that he would permit us to go out of the room, and talk it over. My problems had been caused by my childhood, and not by employment, so there was little chance of a successful claim in that direction. My Attorney and I talked this over, but it didn't take long come to the conclusion that I should accept this offer. The whole hearing probably didn't take more than ten minutes, but now I would have to wait for the Social security to complete the process.

One part of that process was an assessment by a clinical psychologist. They made an appointment with the same man that I had seen in late 1993, and we did very well. This was on the twenty second of April. It rained all day.

For some time to come I would be trying to figure out what my new lifestyle should be like. I knew that I would not do well in an apartment situation. I could either rent an apartment, and move every month or two, or I could stay on the street, and rent an apartment at the same time. (I could use the apartment to take showers, keep stuff in, take shelter in bad weather, and once in a while have a hot meal.) I could also do something else. More on this later.

I wasn't at all sure about all this off the street stuff, so I planned to set up yet another shelter back on the island that I first camped on. To this end I started moving boards to the jetty where the boat was stolen.

On tenth of May, I went to the landing near the businesses early in the morning. Lo and behold, someone had left the lock off their shed. I looked it over and didn't see anything obviously wrong, so I locked it, and went about my business.

I went by there later and told them what I had done. They had one of these services that check your property when you are not there. I guess I got them and the man who was supposed to lock the shed in trouble. Oh well. They were super to let me lock my Kayak to their fence, and it was the least I could do to lock up their shed. Nothing was taken.

The rest of the day was taken up with buying shoes, helping a friend with his lawn mowers, and grocery shopping. My friend gave me two pair of shoes, one of which I gave to my Father. At a rummage sale I bought a daypack for twenty-five cents. It was a really nice pack, but someone had ripped out one of the straps. I sewed it in later, and still have it. I also sent letters to my Father, and a friend.

For the next month I just waited, and survived. I did the usual things, shopping, buying books, reading the entertainment ones, and studying the serious ones. I was preparing for a lot of eventualities, including being homeless some more.

In mid June I was still getting set to make a new shelter, so I did the usual things, make trails, and accumulate lumber. I had already done some of this, but now I was making a real effort. The days were longer, and the weather was better. By this time I had little trust in the bureaucracies or the social service agencies, which is why I was preparing for yet another year as a homeless person.

In late June I came down with a head cold, This would last for a week or more, and slow me down. I am thankful that I had so few illnesses when I was homeless, and most of those were not serious.

On the twenty fourth of June I made the last check on the fire watch job. If they hadn't called by this time they weren't going to. There was no point in making any further demands on my invisibility situation, in going back and forth so frequently, or on the Community Action peoples resources.

On the second of July, I made a midnight move of boards. The reason for this was that there was a very high tide that night, and I could float the boards off much easier, and float them in much closer than a usual tide. I made two loads that night, and went to bed, but didn't stay there very long. I had to get up at 3:15 AM and go to town! That's the way the tides worked. By this time it's the third of July. The tide that I moved the boards on was the same tide that I went to town on, because it was so high, it lasted longer.

When I checked at the Post Office box, the determination from the Social Security Administration had arrived. I was disabled. (I knew that!!!)I had to wait all day for the tide to come back in, but at least I would have some security in the world, but not much. I remembered how quickly the State of Oregon had changed their minds. Who can trust these people?

It could be months before I would see any money. I called my Attorney to see if the process of starting my benefits could be speeded up. I did this on the ninth of July. I was told to make an appointment with the Social Security people, and they could speed things up. Normally it would take about four months before your benefits started, but if you were on the street they would speed things up.

I had seen a helicopter fluttering around a few days before, but I never expected what happened on the tenth of July. I had visitors, four Policemen. It seemed that the ketch weed that grew near my shelter looked like marijuana from the sky. They looked everything over, and told me that because I had a clean camp they would not tell me to leave, but I had to check with the Port of Coos Bay. They said that they would put in a good word for me. The tides were wrong for me to go to town just then, but I started packing anyway.

On the next day I went to town and called the Port people. They said that I had to leave and to remove my shelter as well. I was to be gone by the next Monday. This was Thursday. So I made arrangements to get a storage unit, and walked all over town to get everything together. This was the day that I made the appointment with the Social Security people.

When I got back to camp I was in a hurry. I had to pack up to leave, and I had to take down my shelter, and pack it to the nearest drift area. I also had to carry all my things to a suitable area that I could hide them in, and yet that was close to where I had to load them up into the boat. I wanted to be out of there by Saturday, not Sunday, so it was time to work myself. The distance to the drift area was not far, but I had a lot to carry, and so it was quite a chore. I knew I couldn't go back to the old camp on the other island, because that island had the same situation as the one I was on. The only thing I could do is to go back to the old camp, north of the cities.

The next day was the twelfth of July, and I had a lot to do. I first tore down the shelter, and started moving the stuff that I wanted to go to the storage unit, to the landing area. That day I moved about forty percent of the boards from the shelter to the drift area. I spent the night in the tent, near the landing area. My log says that I was VERY tired.

The next day I finished moving the boards to the drift area early. I had not used up all my firewood last winter, so I had to pack that too. It took several loads to get the things to the place where I could load them in the cab. I called a cab, and loaded it up, and then we went to my storage unit. I had lunch in town, then back to the island. I had to wait till the tide came in to get the things that I needed in the old camp. I made six loads with the Kayak, then called the cab again. They had a station wagon cab, and I specified that this was the vehicle I wanted sent. The cab dropped my things and I on the road as close as possible to my old camp.

The next day I was faced with packing all that stuff up the hill AGAIN. I had a lot of other things to do too. I got a ride into town with my mushroom picking friend, thanks again. I had to wait two hours until the tide came in, then I went to the island. I picked up some items, and some boards, then paddled my boat for the last time to my friends place. I cleaned the boat, helped my friend with some bikes he was fixing, did some grocery shopping, and walked the ten miles or so back to camp. I carried two more loads of things up the hill, and called it a day.

The next day was the sixteenth, and my appointment with the Social Security people, about my benefits. They said that because the checks had all been made out for that month I wouldn't get any money until late the next month. Oh well, there would be more money when I got it.

I opened a bank account the same day, so they could direct deposit my monthly benefits. They still had to start the money with a check, don't ask me why. From there I went to my storage unit with some items that I didn't need in my camp.

My friend had given me a bike, so I rode it back to camp, but had quite a detour in the process. I was riding the bike along the sidewalk, about halfway between Coos Bay and North Bend, when a man in a pickup stopped in front of me. He said that he had just bought a van, and needed someone to drive it to Eugene for him. He would give me twenty dollars to do it, and pay my expenses. I wasn't doing anything right then, so I said OK.

What he didn't tell me was that he wanted me to help him load it with scrap copper first! All this for twenty dollars!

We got some of it loaded, but the van had an engine problem, it smoked very badly. It was burning oil at such a rate that when you hit the gas, the world disappeared. After the first, or second stop to pick up metal, one of the spark plugs fouled. It had a six-cylinder motor, and now only was running on five. The man told me to drive it back to where we had picked it up, because he wanted his money back.

After he had gotten his bucks back, we had to unload the metal into his pickup, and go get a rental trailer to haul the additional metal that he wanted to get. I worked nearly three hours what with all this, and wanted to be paid for my labor.

He said, "All I've got is a twenty-dollar bill."

I figured the amount he owed me was fourteen dollars. He wasn't going to pay me anything, but I had gotten his address when we thought that we were going to Eugene. I told him that I knew where he lived, and would file a complaint with the state labor people. I had six dollars, and so made change. What a deal.

I had changed my address that day, to the Postal Station in Pony Village Mall. We had left my bike there, and I had to walk the half-mile to the bike from where he had left me. What a day, what a week. PTL!

My friends where I landed the boat, were going to have a yard sale, so this seemed a good time to sell the Kayak. I went to their place on Friday the nineteenth, to get things ready. Saturday and Sunday were the sale days, but except for the boat, I didn't take much in. I got $175.00 for the boat. I didn't need it any more, and the storage unit was too small to keep it in. The other storage unit I had had before was twice as large. There was another consideration as well, the Social Service agencies would consider it resources, and require it be sold before I could get food stamps, or benefits.

On Thursday the twenty fifth of July, I packed my washing to town. While I was at the Laundromat, I called the people that had the van I had been driving for my former employer. When I was there I had heard what the price was.

I asked them if they still had it, and they said, "Yes." I asked them if the price was the same as it was, and they said, "Yes." So after I finished doing my wash I called a cab, and went over and bought it. The price was $82.50. It was ugly, and rusted out in places, but after extensive repairs it has been a reliable means of transportation for about five years. I later used it for parts on another van.

The rest of the day was spent transferring my things from the storage unit, to the van. Then I changed the title on the van to my name. I helped a friend of mine with a lawn mower, and then I took a cab back to the bridge, from which I walked back to camp. I had left the van at a friend's of mine back yard. I told him that I would have it out of there before September.

By this time I've come to some conclusions about the way I need to live after my homeless period: I need to be in a situation where if I'm feeling hassled by others emotional demands, I can move QUICKLY. I once had a van/travel trailer combination, and now I've got the front half. If I can buy a travel trailer that is reasonably decent, for about three thousand dollars, I can make this happen. The van, because of the six-cylinder motor, will not pull a large trailer. I will have to use something that is between eighteen and twenty-two feet long, and self contained.

I already know about how much money I will have. If I had not had the delay in my getting the hearing, I would be getting about forty two hundred dollars less than I would otherwise would. Like Jacob in the book of Genesis, the Lord did not allow them to hurt me. I got quite a lot more than that, but some other money was going to have to go to fix up the van. (The cost of the van fix would come to about seventeen hundred dollars, and I did all the wrench bending.) There were other expenses as well.

I know that I will be getting the money in late August, so now it's time to go shopping. The time is mid August, and it takes a lot of walking, but I do find some units that may prove to be suitable, and some that won't. One of the suitable ones was still there when I finally got the benefits.

On the nineteenth of August, I made a marathon

127

walk around the North Spit. I walked about seven and a half-hours, and came back with a lot of things. Some of the things I could use myself, others I could sell, so others could use them.

August the twenty first was a red-letter day; the back benefits check had finally arrived! For a moment or two I just looked at the check. I said to myself, now why did I do this? I would find out a year or so later that it is common for people who have been on the street for a long time to have second thoughts about changing their lifestyles.

It would be a day or so after I deposited it before I could spend it. I still had about five hundred dollars left from when I was getting welfare, so I could get things started.

I spent the next night in a motel. The next day was spent figuring out what to do about the engine, get a new one, or buy a used one. I got insurance on the van, and then went to the Department of Motor Vehicles, and got registration and tags for the plates. Now I could drive!

The van interior was a mess, and the engine was filthy, so I cleaned the engine at the car wash, and plowed and harrowed the inside of the van. I got rid of the big chunks that way. The van had been used for a delivery vehicle for a radiator and glass shop.

The ashtray was overflowing onto the engine cover, and when I cleaned it up, I found quite a bit of change. What a mess, I wanted to use it to camp in until I got the trailer.

The front tires were junk, so the next stop was the tire store. From there I went to the wrecking yard. They said that they had an engine, and a door. I bought the door for the front and installed it right then. The old one had the bottom of the door rusted off. The engine checked out OK, so I ordered it removed from the vehicle it was in. After my Father's experience I don't buy engines with out checking them out first, and that means hearing them run. I listen to them with a screwdriver to ear method, like in stethoscope no less. That way I can tell if they have internal problems.

I picked up some items that I had stashed at my friend's place, and went to the bottom of the hill nearest my camp. I made three loads down the hill that night, and rented a spot in one of the local parks, near the Airport. I camped in the van that night, frugal me.

The next day was the twenty-third, a Friday. I thought that I had better have a place to park the trailer before I got it, so I put in an application at a trailer/RV park. I didn't have any rental references, so I used some of my friends as character references.

The next step was to buy a trailer, so I went to the place that I had looked at them before, and bought one. It was twenty-one feet long, and self-contained. At that time it was eighteen years old, and looked good, and was reasonably clean inside.

The next step was to get the parts needed to fix the brakes on the van, the brakes weren't going to quit yet, but needed attention. The next stop on my automotive agenda was the appointment I had made at the front-end shop. I had lunch, and killed time, but when I got I back to the front-end shop, it hadn't been done. When I asked them why, they said that the tie rods, and the drag link were junk. This was something I had forgotten to check.

I called the trailer park to find out if I had been accepted, and I was! I went out there and paid the rent on the trailer space. From there I went back to the place where I had purchased the trailer, and made arrangements to have it delivered.

The rest of the day was spent shopping, and packing another three loads down from my old camp. Once again I spent the night in the park, near the Airport.

The next day was Saturday, and I had a lot to do. It would be a while before the people where I bought the trailer would be ready to move it, so I went shopping. Then I went to the trailer peoples place, and showed them where the trailer had to go. Now I had a home.

There was still much to do. Over the next few weeks I would; change the van motor at my Fathers place, replace the back half of the exhaust system, replace the steering parts that were defective, bolt down the front seat that was flopping around, equip the van to pull the trailer, and take care of a lot of odds and ends. Some of those odds and ends included moving the rest of my stuff out of the camp, and I also discovered that my used motor did not have as good oil pressure as I thought it ought to. I replaced the rod, and main bearings, and the oil pump, no more problems. It still has good oil pressure, over four years later. (The van lasted until January of 2002. In May of that year I bought another van with the same body style, and used parts off the first van to fix van #2.)

The next day was Sunday, and was I ready for a rest. I finally have a place where I don't have to wonder if the Police are going to tell me to leave. Now I have a LICENSE TO LIVE.

The Last Chapter

The Lord was with me in all the situations in which I found myself. I had food, money to do wash, and money to travel. Most of all I had money to buy the books I needed to figure out my personality. I found things, such as gloves, clothes, a watch, and tools to fix things, a lot of which I have yet. Many of these items arrived in such a timely fashion as to indicate providential help, including the van. For all these and much more I can be truly thankful. I had good health for the most part, and the times that I really needed good weather, (When I had to move off the island after the boat was stolen, and when I got it back.) I had it.

With the little surprises I had from the bureaucrats, I'm surprised I got off the street at all. I described in a previous chapter the problems I had getting into the State of Oregon's disability program. I am now going to add some things I learned since.

When I made the appointment at the psychologist's office, The Senior and Disabled Services receptionist told me that they would have someone pick me up. I found, (Much later.) that they don't pick anyone up unless they can call first. So, considering my situation, either someone blew it, or someone made a deliberate attempt to keep me out of their system. By the grace of God I had made arrangements considerably in advance of the time when I was to be at the Psychologists office. With the help of a local business letting me use their telephone, I got my caseworker to come and pick me up.

The next week when the next appointment was due, no one showed. The caseworker said he would be there, So I walked real fast, and got there with three minutes to spare. (If you don't keep your appointments, you are not working with the program.) The caseworker said, "I forgot." Well maybe. Twice in a row gives me cause to wonder. In spite off all this I still got into the program. I was not a happy camper when I got to the psychologist's office. I felt abandoned. Relationships are a mater of trust, and to have been betrayed like this did set the stage for what happened in 1995, when they pulled that stunt with the reassessment process.

The process of getting into the Social Security program too is burdened with pitfalls. (One example is this; if you do any work at all, even mow a lawn, they toss your case. You, of course, can re-file at any time. The time you spent waiting is lost. I'm sure they would tell you if you asked, but they won't tell you otherwise.)

You have to be assessed then reassessed, and then you have a hearing with a Judge. When I got to the reassessment process, I wanted to find out what they had determined about my personality, with the intention of using this information to work on my problems. So I asked the caseworker to let me look at them. (This didn't happen.) So instead of sending on the file, she put it in the drawer of her desk and forgot it. I called to find out what had happened, and lo and behold, I had waited two months for nothing.

When I asked to do this I should have been told what would happen, and all the possible situations that would result. The key to working with a system is understanding how it works. You are not going to know unless they tell you, if you are not told you'll be messed up. Not much fun when you are out in the cold! I don't think it was deliberate, she was just an airhead, and spaced it. I was mad, and never spoke to her again. After that I just went to the front desk when I wanted to find out something about my case. She did try to speed up the process, but it didn't do much good.

The problem seems to be that no consideration is given to the situation of the person who comes to the bureaucrat for service. No one realizes that a homeless person is in a survival situation, and that to make a phone call he needs to talk to a person. The message on the machine that they will call back, would be funny, except that may have been all the change he or she had. The result is that that I've got small patience with telephone answering machines. I wouldn't have one of the things.

I'm sure that countless caseworkers have been angered when the homeless person didn't keep their appointment. A look out the window would have told them why. It was raining, snowing, cold, or some other kind of bad weather was keeping them in whatever shelter they had found. The first duty of a person is to survive, so they are faced with a cruel choice, sacrifice their eventual benefit for their immediate survival. I always kept my appointments, with one exception, but sometimes it was tough.

It looks as though we need a system that will be flexible enough to deal with the homeless person when he or she comes in. You need to bear in mind that a person that has mental or emotional problems, may never return to the office. In order to treat a homeless person properly, you need to treat them as if they are in the emergency room. This is a emergency situation, the threat to their health is very real. Having them wandering around like that is not good for them or society. They will probably be picked up and jailed for some petty, or not so petty crime, when all they needed was timely help. (Some would have to be supervised anyway.) It costs taxpayers far more to jail someone, (About three times as much.) as it does to support them in the Social Security system, not to mention the cost to the victims of such crimes. The purpose of government is to protect its citizens. I would seem, once again, that an ounce of prevention would equal a pound of cure.

The problem is the wait, people can do desperate acts if they feel uncared for. The bureaucracies feel that all should be for their convenience. (It is very inefficient to have people standing around doing nothing, or so busy that they have to stay long after normal working hours.) The result is not good for those who have immediate needs. I checked with my attorney in November of 2000, and was informed that it takes about two years to process a claim in the Social Security system. Mine took about twenty months, then add on two months for lost paperwork, and nine months because I felt hassled. (In April of 2002 Peter Jennings on ABC News reported that it now took three years to get disability through the Social Security System.)

One effect that the lack of a rent receipt may have is

lack of sleep. In this society you are not supposed to sleep unless you have a legal right to do so. This results in sleep deprivation, which is a form of torture. Torture, prolonged, can have a variety or results, hopelessness, (Alienation) uncaring attitudes toward self and others, violence, and more than I either know or could list. I didn't have this problem, as I always made my camps in difficult to get to locations, and so got enough sleep.

Another problem is lack of an address. I didn't have too much trouble in this, as I had loyal friends who let me use theirs. It is difficult to keep up with a case situation if you don't have a P.O. box, or other address were mail can be received. Because I had an address in Oregon, I was allowed to rent a P.O. Box. It would still be possible to go to the Social Security office and check on the progress of your case, but would be difficult because of the difficulty in getting there. Some welfare offices will allow you to pick up food stamps and welfare checks on a walk in basis. Once again transportation is the problem.

The time situation is the main problem. In the time it takes to process your claim you can, die, be criminalized, or be moved out by the Police. (To have to go to another city, which will delay processing.) Plus all the psychological effects which have already been discussed. The person may even get used to street life, and although they may say that they want to get off the street, when it comes to it, they don't. (When I got off the street I chose a lifestyle as close as possible to the way I lived when I was on the street.)They must be gotten off the street quickly, or they may be lost to normal society. This is not good for them or society. The effect of all this is that the Social Security people are running a concentration camp without walls. I hope this is not deliberate, but that is the result.

You may be asking yourself, "Isn't that a little ex-treme?" So let's make a statement of principle; the only way a person can die or be debilitated, (Other than natural causes, suicide or murder.) Is when someone who is RESPONSIBLE for him or her, fails to provide basic needs in a timely fashion. In some of the Nazi concentration camps of WW II they killed people outright, but in others they just didn't feed them enough, or provide sufficient shelter. The Congress of the U.S.A. has made the Social Security Administration responsible for disabled persons.

I used to sing and play the guitar, but after all those years out in the cold my voice is about as musical as a crow's. Some of those years were before I applied for benefits, but some of them weren't. In early 1995, I was diagnosed with a bowel restriction, which will eventually turn out to be fatal. The Doctor gave me a program of therapy, which will prolong my life. One of the things that he said to avoid was stress. Some of that stress could be attributed to the life I was leading. One thing I found out through my studies, is that, if you have emotional problems, sooner or later they will show up somewhere in your physical self. The situation I was in contributed heavily to this negative physical problem. Other than that I don't know of any other problems that were caused by the wait while Social Security people processed my claim. (The condition has improved to the point that my Dr. said that I won't need another check up for five years. PTL!)

It's like this, one man says to another, "What's the instrument that man is playing?" (Not to well either.) The next man says, "That's the violin." Then the first man says, "Well then what's he doing fiddling around with it." They are fiddling around with our lives! I think we are going to have to have major changes before we can get the job done.

I know that it's no good to criticize without making some positive suggestion, so here it is, camps. They should be, well maintained, with counseling, security, (Cheap laundry too, dimes instead of quarters, or free.) public transportation, on site social services, and with a comprehensive policy of putting the homeless person first.

The camp would be of individual shelters with some kind of heat, and capable of being cleaned with a fire hose. They would not have amenities like electric lights, unless as a special privilege for work around the camp, or if there were school children. They could be made modular for families. (Just move in a room with a forklift, then adjust to fit a doorway in one end of the dwelling. The other end has the entrance.)

These dwellings would be modeled on the shelters I used when I was homeless, but instead of using a tarp, some kind of opaque roofing could be used. Climate would be a factor in heating and insulation. There would be many problems to be overcome, zoning regulations, unfriendly neighbors, and sewage being a few. The alternative, however, is to let people die or be neglected, which I feel is unacceptable in a civilized society. I've been there myself and I know how it feels.

This solution would not work for everybody. (Such as myself.) People that need to be alone a lot would find this situation intolerable. You would get negative results if you tried to force them, or anyone into this situation. This needs to be a free choice, not one coerced by the local law enforcement agencies.   Persons wanted by the law, or burdened with guilt, would be difficult to help as well. The camp idea would be a step in the right direction, a large step, but would not cure it all.

One of the advantages of the Social Security system is this; when you finally do get your money, you get all those back benefits. (Less what the local state gets back for the welfare they paid you.) This amount can be a tidy sum. I know in my own case that it took about six thousand dollars to get me off the street. I'm still using the situation that I selected for myself.

The unfortunate part of this is, that no one councils the new recipient as to the best use for all this nice money. You can only have an amount over two thousand dollars for six months, then they stop your benefits. They will reinstate them as soon as the amount falls below the above figure. I met some people who had just gotten their benefits, and they lived pretty high for a while.

If you were only in the present system for a few weeks, the cash available would be minimal. So an award amount would have to be made, and counseling would have to be given, both depending upon the condition and abilities of the person involved. (Some would never be able to get off the street. They would not be able to keep themselves or

136

their dwelling clean, would make too much noise, etc. In a word they are not housebroken. Whether this could remedied with training or not I don't know.)

It is possible that an otherwise viable individual might be refused housing because of no references. The only way to solve this problem is to slip a very large sum of money under the table to the manager of a potential location. Unless this money is made available the person is still going to be homeless. Safeguards would have to be in place, so someone would not use the money for something else. All this may sound like a lot to do, but the result should be positive. People like myself who <u>must </u>be alone, should be helped to find a situation in which they will not feel abused. I like my solution, so, whenever I feel hassled, I just turn the key, and no more hassle. That would not work for everybody, however.

If you are reading this to see what the hassles of homeless people are, and thus be more accepting of them, or you are reading this to find how God can be present, and work, no mater what your situation, good. I suspect, however, that there are some that will be reading this to further disadvantage those who are called homeless. If that is the case I pray that the Lord God Almighty rebuke you for your attitude, and publicly humiliate you for your action. I will further pray that through this chain of circumstances you will repent of your attitudes, and actions, and come to a saving knowledge of the Lord Jesus Christ. I know that I, too, had some attitudes that needed changing before the Lord got a hold of me. I thought that war was a good thing, got rid of the excess population. I no longer think that way, thank God.

When you are on the street you can loose your sense of belonging, you feel always on the defensive. You must, at all costs, avoid the question, "Where do you live." I didn't lie, as that is contrary to my faith. usually just told them I had a "special" situation. I'm sure some of them guessed, people are not stupid, but they didn't KNOW. Since I've gotten off the street I find I am comfortable parking my wheels about as far away from the store as I can get. I trace this behavior to the feeling that, without a rent receipt, I have no right to be there. I used to do this without thinking, but I am getting better, after I analyzed my behavior. (Even though I have a rent receipt now, I still have a tendency to do this.) Truly a rent receipt is a LICENSE TO LIVE.

In this book I have dumped on the social agencies that kept me alive. Some may consider this ungrateful, but if you leave someone out in the cold, the homeless person may feel more abused than grateful.

Because I have dumped on them they may try to give me a black eye too. After all if someone makes someone look bad one way of drawing attention from yourself is to make him look bad too. I consider that this could be the price for telling the truth. If it happens so be it.